To Fran
With Best
Love

Chris

CW00454844

WILLIAM CATCOTT

THE COMPLETE WORKS

Edited by
Clare Blackmore, Bill Allen,
and Sarah Wride

Illustrated by Wendy Lovegrove

WALTON PRESS · GLASTONBURY
2018

First edition published in the UK, 2018. ISBN: 978-1-5272-2137-6

Printed and bound in the UK by Walton Press Ltd, Glastonbury.
Printed on FSC accredited materials.

For Bill Allen, a true gentleman.
(30 March 1942 – 25 March 2018)

CONTENTS

Editorial Procedure..i
A Memoir of William Catcott..ii

Rural Pleasure..1
Childhood...2
To the *Wells Journal*..3
Life...4
We Rise to Guard our Fatherland..5
The Vacant Chair in the Corner..6
The Memories of Home..7
The Twilight Hour...8
The Last Leaf..9
Spring..10
A Song of Progress...11
The Odd Fellows' response...12
The Shepton Mallet Odd Fellow's Funeral...13
A Patriotic Song..15
The Orphan's Tear...16
Lines on a Beautiful Swan, Barbarously Beaten to Death in the Palace Moat.................18
A Summer Evening Thought..19
Among the Sheaves...20
Onwards..21
The Opening of the Railway to Wells...22
Kindness..24
Musings in the Meadows...25
Summer...27
My Worn Out Barrow..28
A Reverie...30
My Sweet Hawthorn..32
Evening Musing...33
A Sunny Memory...34
Old England...36
The Old Grey Mare..37
The Deserted Bride..40
The Merry Reapers..42
To my Nephew William Henry Catcott in the Army of the Potomac..............43
The Daisy on my Mother's Grave..44
Friendship..45
In Memorium...47
Lines to the Memory of Kit, who was Killed by a Greyhound, 7th October 1847.................48
Lizzie's Pathetic Appeal to Harry..50
To a Primrose, Brought from the Garden of the Cornish Poet........................51
The Bottle..53
Morning...54
Shaded Flowers..56
The Soldier's Prayer..57
Lines Suggested by an Advertisement for a "Maid of All Work"....................58

To a Primrose in the Cathedral Green...60
Sunny Sue's Birthday...61
An Acrostic on the Eminent Lecturer, Linguist and Philanthropist Elihu Burrit...........62
Christmas..63
The Village Churchyard..64
Stanzas Written on Receiving some Primroses from a Friend at Truro...........................65
Emily's Birthday..67
Emma's Birthday..68
Blighted Hopes...69
Words of Welcome...71
Lines on a Picnic Party at Knoll Hill, Shepton Mallet...73
Our Flower Show...75
The Flower Show...76
The Daisy..78
Harvest Home...79
The Thatcher's Daughter..80
November..81
The Drunkard..82
Poor Dobbin's Death..84
John Cross..86
Life in a London Bakehouse..88
The Man and the Moat...90
Song to the Mowing Machine..91
Away with Melancholy...92
To Mary upon Receiving her Photograph..93
Evening...94
Evening Musings..95
The Welcome Redbreast...96
The Widow's Little Boy..97
Autumn...99
The Disappointed Wedding Party..100
Mary Ann's Grave..102
Pious Susan...103
The Sabbath Morn..106
A Word to the Baker's Reply..107
A Baker's Toil...108
Seasonable Stanzas...110
The Rosy Little Bar-Maid..112
May..113
Evening...113
Pretty Polly Fear...114
The Shepton Mallet Odd Fellows' Festival..115
My Village Home..117
The Harvest Again..118
The Robin..119
Autumn Breeze...120
The Cat and her Tormentor...121
The Coming of Age of Charles Clement Tudway...123
To a Primrose in November..124
Reminiscence..125

"One Story's Good till t'other's Told"...126
Dear Little Alfred, Youngest Son of John Harris, the Cornish Poet............................128
Fanny's Gift...129
Drunken Ned's Soliloquy...130
Oh Tell Me Not of Dreary Things...132
Sonnet to William Budd, Esq., M.D., Clifton..134
"Poor Old Parfitt"..135
I'm Sometimes Sad...136
Sixteen Summers...138
March..139
Have Mercy on the Calves..141
The Home Nurse..143
Bonny Bess, the Happy Housemaid...144
An Ode, Written at the West of England Sanatorium, Weston-super-Mare 145
Carrie, the Merry Orphan Maid..146
Our Convalescent Cook..148
Pretty Polly..149
The Plough...151
Poor Old Primrose...152
To a Dear Friend's Firstborn Son..154
Christian Charity..155
Poor Jack...157
To a Violet...159
Winter...160
Early Impressions..161
Lillie Green...163
The Soldier's Betrothed...164
Rain..166
The Water Question...167
The Artful Rustic...169
The Poet's Walk..171
The Early Primrose..173
April..174
Cornish Violets..175
Stanzas to a Friend on Receiving Some Primroses in a Letter....................................176
To Mary...177
An Ode to John Harris, the Cornish Poet...178
The New Year...180

Obituary..183
Index of first lines...184

EDITORIAL PROCEDURE

The poems are published in order of first publication. In 1854 W. and R. George of Sadler Street, Wells published a small volume of Catcott's poems, entitled *Morning Musings*. A second volume, under the same title, was published just before William's death in November 1870; there are, to our knowledge, only three copies of the latter extant. We therefore do not know whether poems published in the *Wells* or *Shepton Mallet Journals*, *Bath* and *Worcestershire Chronicles*, *Cornubian and Redruth Times*, *Bristol Times and Mirror*, and *Morning Musings* (1870) first appeared in *Morning Musings* (1854).

127 of Catcott's poems were first published in journals with different – and changing - house styles, but 79 of these were republished, together with 9 new poems, in *Morning Musings* (1870). To avoid inconsistencies, the text and grammar of each poem has therefore been copied from its last known publication. In "text and grammar" we include different conjugations ("withering" to "withered"), syntax, and wording that does not alter the line's meaning ("and sweeter for the nature's child" to "and dearer far to Nature's child"); excluded changes are footnoted.

Clare Blackmore
Bill Allen
Sarah Wride

i

MEMOIR OF THE AUTHOR

William Catcott was born on February 27th 1808, at [Rock House,] West Horrington, a small village belonging to Wells in the county of Somerset. This village, consisting chiefly of miners' huts, is situated on the southern slope of the Mendip Hills, and here our author learned his first lessons of labour, poetry, and love. His father was a stocking-maker, employing one hand to comb the wool, which, when converted into worsted and hose, he carried in his wallet and sold to such customers as he could find in adjacent towns and villages. Mining, however, was the ruling passion and, it may be added, the bane of his life; for every hour and every shilling he could spare from the stocking business was wasted "on the hill." When very young, William Catcott, who was the elder of several [two] sons [and one sister], went to a dame's school, until he could read tolerably well in the New Testament. He next went to a higher-class school for two winter quarters, acquired a knowledge of writing and arithmetic, learned the mysteries of the multiplication table, and managed to work a sum correctly in simple division. The poet, however, had a good mother, at whose feet he learned the noblest lessons of his life, the lessons of piety, forbearance and industry, which were to fit him for the greater school of the world. He speakers of her as "an exemplary woman and a most affectionate mother." Her father was the clerk of the parish of Binegar, a good musician, composer and singer. "Many a time", he adds, "has my mother delighted us by singing an anthem which her father had finished a few days before his death. She had an excellent voice, and I fancy now, I hear her singing 'Tom Bowling' and 'The Lass of Richmond Hill' as I have never heard them sung since." The poet has recorded a few of the reminiscences of this period in his 'Early Impressions'[.] ...

The cottage library [at West Horrington], composed of such books as a *History of England*, *Robinson Crusoe*, and several religious publications, did but little towards gratifying our poet's inherent love for knowledge. His opportunities, likewise, were but few; for, being the eldest boy, his father required all the assistance the lad could give in the business, and subsequently when mining really commenced, he was entirely occupied with his father "on the hill" – the father in sinking, and the son in drawing over him, frequently worn out with his child-labour before the setting of the sun. In his sixteenth year William went to live with an uncle, a baker, in Wells for the purpose of learning the trade. The baking business, however, not agreeing with his health, he returned at the end of a year to his early village home, and was employed alternately, during the next four years, in the garden, the harvest field and the combing shop. With the view of improving his condition, he now went [at the age of twenty-one] to Kidderminster, where he found employment and very small pay as a wool-comber. During his stay in that town, William's father took a small Mendip farm, and consequently required his son's assistance in the fields. Again, therefore, William returned to rural life, but only for a short time, as he was desirous, like many a young man before him, of seeing the great Metropolis.

Our author's experiences of farm-life in the locality of the Mendip Hills, will account for the many pleasant passages relating to country scenes and subjects, to be found in this volume, especially in 'Harvest Home' and 'The Plough', - lyrics which every reader of taste must admire for their beauty and completeness.

William Catcott, as previously stated, was naturally desirous of seeing London, and of procuring, if possible, some employment of a more remunerative nature than either that of farm-labour, mining, or wool-combing and so, on one fine morning he left the shadows of the Mendip Hills for the mazy streets of the great town. After unsuccessfully pacing the pavement for nine days, he was glad to accept a single-hand place in a baker's shop, for his bed, bread, and thirteen shillings a week. Hours of labour from midnight until six o'clock the following evening. This life of drudgery lasted between two and three years up until the sudden death of his uncle [in Wells]. He now left London for Wells for the purpose of superintending the trade in the very shop where he first learned to mould the "staff of life", and where he still resides. It will be seen, therefore, that William Catcott is a genuine working man in the truest sense of the term, being one of those useful citizens who think and act for the elevation and support of their fellow men. His calling compels him to labour, almost incessantly, for the principal of our physical necessities in the unpoetical and ungenial atmosphere of a bakehouse, yet, in his warm leisure, or when serving his customers in the streets of Wells, or supplying the cottagers in the cool green lanes in the outskirts of the city, the cheery note of a thrush and robin, or a Spring violet among the dry leaves, or a primrose in the grassy confines of the Cathedral Green, or the blue sky mirrored in the face of a stream, awaken pleasant thoughts which, upon the lid of the bread-barrow, or on the boards of the bakehouse, are frequently shaped into graceful and harmonious verse.

The baker, one would imagine from the oppressive nature of his work, could hardly be brought to believe that labour is a Divine provision for the healthful exercise of the perceptive and physical faculties; yet it is so. Our necessities, in accordance with the laws of Providence, compel us to labour, and it is only the want of mutual sympathy between classes that creates unnatural exertion on the one hand and unfruitful indolence on the other. We have only have to look around and see the glory of the fields and the architecture of the city, to learn that labour, guided by thought, is the genius that produces from unconscious materials, all the comforts and elegancies of life. Many occupations, however, such as ploughing and building, afford regular hours for recreation and rest, but the baking trade, in its present condition, admits of little or no real repose for the overwrought system, and scarcely any leisure for the yearnings and aspirations of the soul. The baker's life is one long, Sabbathless round of toil, and the wearisome night-work is the deepest evil with which he has to contend. [In 'A Baker's Toil'] our author very justly pictures from experience, in plain, yet forcible verse, the condition and aspect of these white slaves, the bakers, with which those who have hearts and who love "hot breakfast rolls" will do well thoughtfully to consider[.] …

We think we have said enough by way of introduction to the genial productions of William Catcott, to elicit some public interest in his favour. We have shown that he has had, like many of us, a rough path to travel, but it is the path which makes a man strong in the presence of sunshine and flowers, when, like our baker-poet, he possesses a cheerful and thankful spirit. William Catcott is not only a pleasing verse writer and contributor to the local press, but he is a very useful member of society, although the Committee of the Wells Literary and Scientific Institute, in consequence of an outspoken poem which appeared, some years ago, in the *Bath Journal*, refused their townsman a card of membership; he is also benevolent and kind-hearted, aiding, as far as he is able by his life and writings, every good cause which tends to the real advancement of people.

We conclude our imperfect notice of the author of this interesting volume with the beautiful ode, written by John Harris, the Cornish miner-poet, and addressed William Catcott, on his birthday, February 27th, 1865: -

"There was a golden time, I ween,
When ivy bright, or laurel green,
From woodland copse, or pastoral glen,
Or hedgerow high, or murmuring fen,
As birthdays opened fresh and clear,
Adorned the brow of bardie dear.

"Those days are gone! The singer now
Gets scarce a leaflet for his brow.
No laurels cluster round his head,
But Sorrow's weeds are there outspread,
Bound by Neglect's cold fingers drear,
Upon the brow of bardie dear.

"Yet he is Nature's favourite son,
Her greatest, grandest, choicest one:
Her mysteries are by him revealed,
Her secrets are by him unsealed,
Nor loves she mid her votaries here,
None like her own, her bardie dear.

"She teaches with her flower and weed:
Her book is more than college creed.
She rears up poets here and there,
Like golden ores on flat lands bare.
With tongues of winds and brooklets clear,
She makes her own sweet bardie dear.

"What had the bard to do with schools,
　　Or tedious academic rules?
He finds his idyls where the breeze
Walks like a prophet through the trees.
The bud, the flower, the last leaf sere,
　　All teach the true-born bardie dear.

"Were there no lichened rock or stone,
　　No solemn ruin, moss-o'ergrown,
　　No village lane, no stream or rill,
　　No footpath winding round the hill,
　　No moor where larks delight the ear,
　　Small claim had I to bardie dear.

"What taught thee in thy native Wells,
　　But Nature's language in her dells,
　　By daisy-mead, or hillock's brow?
Hence thy sweet lyric to 'The Plough,'
　　Replete with rural echoes clear,
　　Delicious to the bardie dear.

"So let me bind thy brow to-day,
　　Not with green laurel, but a lay,
Which gushes from a grateful heart,
That takes in song a pleasant part,
And wish thee many a tuneful year,
And crown thee Nature's bardie dear."

John Blackman, 1870[1]

---

[1] Catcott's friend and fellow rural poet; Blackman was born in Cobham in Surrey and emigrated to Australia in 1870.

RURAL PLEASURE

Oh! where the stream flows o'er the pebbles clear,
And charms with music sweet the listening ear,
Where blooms the violet and the primrose pale,
Adown the lovely, elm-clad sheltered vale;
Where nature ever wears her mantle green,
And rural beauty glows in every scene;
Where zephyrs sing to rest the dying day,
Far from the city's smoke and din away;
There let me ramble oft at day's decline,
And cheerful homage pay at natures' shrine;
There muse awhile on that mysterious power,
Which lights the stars and paints the fragrant flower;
There close my eye, and view the spirit-land,
And crush the cares of life with Fancy's wand.

Bath Journal, 1850

CHILDHOOD

What memories the feelings greet,
When glancing through the mist of years,
So that brief day of Childhood gay,
Undimmed by ripened manhood's tears!

Whene'er we trace our rapid race,
From rosy youth to years mature,
That dear old spot is ne'er forgot,
'Tis stamped on memory's tablet sure.

The flowers that grew when life was new,
Were sweeter, fairer, then than now;
Each scene was bright, and with delight,
We revelled with a careless brow.

Where'er we roam, my early home
Still gleams before the mental eye;
And as we toil through life's turmoil
The homeward glance oft prompts the sigh.

Oh yes! 'twas there beneath the care
Of parents dear we frolicked wild,
And plucked the flowers of young life's hours,
While sunny faces on us smiled.

Our hearts were light with visions bright
Of brighter seasons yet to come;
With lavish hand new joys we planned,
While seated round our hearth at home.

Though getting old, for years have rolled
Us near and nearer to life's close,
Our native hill looks lovely still,
Gemmed with the myrtle and the rose.

We've toiled along the thorns among,
And sometimes seen our labours blest;
And cheered by Hope adown life's slope,
We march towards our promised rest.

Bristol Times and Mirror, January 1851

TO THE *WELLS JOURNAL*[1]

Go forth thou herald of a brighter day
Speed on, with all the force and charm of youth
And scatter o'er the lands the seeds of truth.
Go, aid the sons of toil and pave the way
For their progression to the destined end,
And to the slave thy ready succour lend.
Go, fearless to the proud oppressor's gate,
And boldly there they onward mission state.
Go, and proclaim aloud thy rule divine
Which, Honoured makes both prince and peasant shine.
Go, with the sword of justice in thine hand
And with high intent and holy aim,
Expose and drive each tyrant from the land
And give the poor the rights their merits claim.

Wells Journal, August 1851

---

[1] Victorian entrepreneur, Samuel Backhouse, founded the *Wells Journal* in August 1851. To this poem, published in the *Journal*'s second issue, the editor made the following reply: "These are very high aspirations for us. But if due allowance is made for poetic licence, perhaps it might be said that we will do our best".

LIFE

Did you ever think how noble
Is a life upon the earth?
Did you ever scan the reason
The Creator gave you birth?
'Twas because a holy mission
He had for you to fulfil,
And because life's widening river
Needed one more little rill.

Should the tiny streamlet loiter,
Or in marches turn aside?
Should it not then rather hasten
On to swell the flowing tide?
Shall the Heaven-created Spirit
Grovel in the dust of earth,
Shall it not be up and doing,
Worthy of its noble birth?

Never shrink away from duty,
But let your light shine brightly,
Promptly aid your struggling brother,
And scan his errors slightly;
Let the milk of human kindness
Flow in a perennial stream,
And the burning words you utter,
Wake the sluggard from his dream.

For ever present, though unseen,
Spirits from the land above,
The motives of your actions scan,
Shedding on you tears of love!
While men and Angels watch you,
Let your thoughts and aims be high,
Leave a shining track behind you
And the frown of fools defy.

Life is great! Oh, life is holy!
There is work for you to do,
Ever rising and progressing,
Be you faithful, be you true;
Gently lead the weak and erring
On to power. Light and love;
Be on earth to all a blessing,
Till you rise to spheres above.

Wells Journal, February 1852

4

WE RISE TO GUARD OUR FATHERLAND[2]

We rise to guard our fatherland,
The land where Freedom's banner waves;
Around our homesteads dear, we stand,
Well armed beside our fathers' graves;
Whose spirits, whispering in the breeze
  That stirs the flowers at eventide,
  Allure us from the plains of ease,
To guard the land in which they died.

While beaming from a thousand eyes,
  The smile of beauty cheers us on,
While patriots' prayers ascend the skies,
  And home is dear to sire and son,
We'll firmly stand and face the foe,
Whene'er he dares to cross the main,
  And with our rifles bravely show
How much we prize our old domain.

From every hill our flag shall wave,
  From every dell a shout ascend,
From every hearth shall march the brave,
  And every class in union blend;
Woe to the foe who dares to tread
The hallowed soil where freedmen dwell;
  A gory grave shall be his bed,
And Briton's shouts his funeral knell.

Wells Journal, August 1862

---

[2] Written for the Wells Volunteer Rifle Brigade, which provided support for the regular army in times of war. It was set to music by Mrs Purnell, wife of Dr. Purnell, who saw to Wells' medical needs and, as the local Officer for Health, reported to the City Council, and has since been published by Robert Cooks and Company.

THE VACANT CHAIR IN THE CORNER

I see the empty chair, but where
Oh! where is he that used to sit
In that snug, cosy corner there,
And charm us with his genial wit?
Stored with the lore of by-gone years,
Called from the city and the dell,
He sipped his ale, forgot his cares,
And told his treasured stories well.

Down there he sat at eventide,
I seem to see him smiling yet,
With Lillie chatting by his side,
And 'neath his chair his faithful pet:
Poor *Tiny* died and little *Mirt*
Became his constant walking mate,
She tripped along through dust and dirt,
And guarded well the corner-seat.

Through dark as well as sunny days,
His chequered course through life had been;
He had his own peculiar ways,
And much of life had felt and seen;
But yet, he owned a generous heart,
A dear old Grandpapa was he,
He always took the poor man's part,
And sympathised with poverty.

I gaze upon the vacant chair,
Beside the window near the fire,
Until the tear-drops, warm and clear,
Run glistening down my trembling lyre;
Whilst thoughts of merry moments gone,
On fancy's pinions borne along,
Give to the heart a sadder tone,
And cast their shadow on my song.

I see him in the chair again!
The words he spoke I seem to hear,
And feel them stealing through my brain,
And think his spirit must be near.
A loving friend who can forget?
Though absent and for ever gone,
The spirit seems to linger yet,
To hold communion with our own.

Wells Journal, December 1852

THE MEMORIES OF HOME

There is one spot to me more dear
Than any 'neath the starry skies,
'Tis ever present, bright and fair,
Fraught with affection's tenderest ties,
A village on a sunny slope
Of one of Mendip's famous hills,
Where my young heart was trained to cope
With opening life's attendant ills.

In white-washed cots, its gardens neat,
Its old familiar faces dear,
In shady lanes and flowerets sweet,
Oft drew my wandering footsteps there;
Its landscape, stretching far away,
And bounded by the silvery tide,
How oft I've viewed at close of day,
With all a native Briton's pride!

Its hedgerow, too, of apples wild,
That ripened on the heath-clad steep,
Tempting many a rosy child,
To toddle thro' the village deep;
And, oh, that sparkling little stream,
So sweetly flowing down the dell,
In memory's tablet brightly gleam,
And make the heart with rapture swell.

And oft my longing eye will turn
Toward the hill my father trod,
Where daisies bloomed beside the fern,
And minerals glittered 'neath the sod;
Where borne upon the evening breeze,
The sheep bells tinkled in my ear,
And thrushes on its bordering trees,
Poured forth their music soft and clear.

The land beyond the Western sea,
They say can boast of prospects grand,
Of noble institutions free,
And commerce crowding on its strand;
Yet, fairer, brighter, in my eyes,
Is that sweet spot on Mendip's side,
With all its hallowed memories,
Than any in the world beside.

Wells Journal, July 1853

THE TWILIGHT HOUR

There's something in the twilight hour
More charming than the glare of day,
When fragrant zephyrs fan the bower,
And birds pour forth their evening lay;
'Tis then the care-worn spirit feels
A soothing sense of calm delight,
A holy influence o'er it steals,
And makes it teem with fancies bright.

How sweet to strike the trembling lyre,
Beside the stream where willows wave,
And kindle there devotion's fire,
And muse on realms beyond the grave;
To watch the stars, the eyes of night
In glory twinkling in the sky,
And, musing on those worlds of light,
Feel lost in silent ecstasy!

In that calm hour, how sweet to think
That life has sunny, happy days,
And fountains pure where all may drink
And give the Lord of Nature praise;
Though threatening clouds may sometimes lower
And cast their shadows on our way,
The sun that shone before the shower,
Will shine when it has passed away.

And though the sunny days of youth
Are now for ever fled and gone,
Those happy days, when love and truth
In all their winning lustre shone?
The present with its shades of cares,
His glorious gleams of sunshine too,
Its mornings fresh, and evenings fair,
Its prospects ever bright and new.

And while Hope paints the coming hours
With hues more dazzling than the last,
How sweet to dream amongst the flowers,
The future will outshine the past;
And muse with rapture on the day
Destined to end the spirit's strife,
And give it wings to soar away
To realms of endless light and life.

Bath Chronicle, October 1853

THE LAST LEAF[3]

The last leaf quivers in the breeze
And trembles on the naked bough,
And through the hollow bending trees,
The wintry blast is howling now.

Yet closely to the spray it clings,
And flutters while the branches sway;
But like the rest of earthly things,
Alas! T'will soon be blown away.

So friends, when adverse breezes blow
Will oft their final exit make,
Like withered leaves they fall below,
And every tie of friendship break.

Unsheltered like the last leaf now
The upright soul oft bears the blast,
Till like the leaf torn from the bough
It yields, and upwards flies at last.

Wells Journal, October 1853

---

[3] This poem was set to music and sung in Wells Cathedral: "Mr Silas Fletcher, to whose musical compositions we have previously had occasion to allude has just published a seasonable song entitled 'The Last Leaf.' Mr. William Catcott, of Tor Street, has furnished the words. The melody is simple and expressive and is in many respects an agreeable echo of the sentiment embodied in the verse. We have no doubt it will contribute to the reputation that the composer has already achieved" (*Wells Journal*, October 1853). Fletcher was a "fashionable boot and shoe maker"; he had a shop in Wells High Street and was a member of the Vicar's Choral. He is buried in Wells Cathedral churchyard.

SPRING

Lovely violets now are blooming
In the forest and the glen,
Brighter prospects, too, are looming
For the toiling sons of men;
Birds are on the hawthorn singing,
Buds are opening on the trees,
Cowslips from the earth are springing,
Bearing honey for the bees.

Gaily in the sun-beam glistening,
Flits the butterfly away,
While the gossamer is streaming
In the merry ploughman's way.
The milkman's voice is ringing,
In the daisy-spangled vale,
And each hour is gladness bringing
To the tenants of the dale.

Swallows o'er the lea are flying,
Trouts are leaping in the stream;
And the bat, when day is dying,
Wakens from its Winter's dream;
The reviving woods are dressing
In their Summer robes again,
And Spring appears with a blessing
For the mountain and the plain.

Nature's sweetest strings are tuning
In the meadow and the grove,
Musing spirits deep communing
With the Deity above;
With new life the earth is teeming,
And the clods so lately bare,
Flora's fingers now are trimming,
Painting meadow, mount, and mere.

God's own bow, high o'er us bending,
Gives to all assurance strong,
That his goodness is unending
To the right and to the wrong;
And the hand that now is leaving
Beauty's impress on each leaf,
Autumn's corn will soon be waving
Ripening the golden sheaf.

Wells Journal, April 1854

A SONG OF PROGRESS

When clouds are low'ring o'er us
The sun-beam then is nigh,
'Tis the falling shower that brings,
The rainbow in the sky.

Then mourn not o'er the changes
Old hoary Time has made
For when the sun shines brightest
The deeper is the shade.

When the billows o'er us break
We'll think upon the brave
That have battled with its might,
And rose upon the wave.

Guided by landmarks sure,
Their struggles have supplied,
Our advancing steps shall be,
To kindred souls a guide.

Undaunted will we train them
To triumph where we won
For deeper is the shadow,
The brighter is the sun.

And priceless will the joy be
To the throbbing breast,
The more severe the labour,
The sweeter is the rest.

Wells Journal, April 1854

THE ODD FELLOWS' RESPONSE[4]

Down from the North the missive came,
The cotton famine was its theme,
And every lodge throughout the land
Prepared to "lend a helping hand"
The wail of want, borne on the breeze,
Swept through the land, and o'er the seas,
And British hearts in every clime,
Beat nobly in that trying time.

Where'er that saddening tale was heard,
The depths of kindred hearts were stirred,
And tears of pity gemmed the eye,
While streams of succour glided by,
Two thousand pounds, aye hundreds more,
They freely voted from the store,
And still, with open hands they stand,
To cheer the needy in the land.

All honour to the brethren then!
God bless these loving, prudent men,
Whose swelling bosoms yearned to prove
The depth of their fraternal love!
Where'er their honoured banner floats,
May glorious deeds and generous thoughts,
Still shed a holy radiance round,
That sunny spot of hallowed ground!

Shepton Mallet Journal, April 1854

---

[4] Overproduction in a time of contracting markets and the interruption of baled cotton during the American Civil War (1861-1865) caused depression in the textile industry; in 1862 the *Wells Journal* printed an appeal from the cotton workers of Lancashire: "Everywhere in the North there is distress. You will find it in the countenance of those being compelled to receive parish relief, by the sight of famished children pinched with hunger. You will find it in the unfurnished rooms, fireless grates, the empty cupboards of hundreds of cottages in which not long ago comfort and contentment reigned. You will find it in the famine fever which is laying prostrate young men and maidens, old men, women and children". "Sermons in aid of the distressed operatives in the North were preached in the Cathedral by the Lord Bishop of the Diocese and at St Cuthbert's by the Rev. J. W. Lace and after an appeal to the Christians £17 12s 6d was collected in the city".

THE SHEPTON MALLET ODD FELLOW'S FUNERAL

Borne on the evening breeze the deep tonn'd knell
Strikes on the listening soul with thrilling power,
And tells once more its oft repeated tale,
That life is short. And while its dismal note
Hangs heavy on the ear, the eye beholds,
A sad corroboration of its truth
In life's mid-day, while yet the eye shone bright
And health's fair bloom was mantling o'er his cheek,
Death hurled its fatal-heaven directed dart,
And smote the sire, the husband and the friend,
And bore his pride away. But ere the spark,
Immortal, paternal kindness sooth'd
Its parting pang and Hope's ethereal beam
Gleamed like a meteor o'er the path it flew
And now midst congregated crowds, is seen
A brother borne by Brothers to the tomb,
Whilst Brothers swell the long funeral train
And follow to the dark sepulchres verge,
The cold remains of one they dearly loved.
Nor is there fond regard extinguished there,
His offspring feel its hallowed warmth,
The Mother's sigh and Orphan's prayers are heard,
And comfort poured into the Widow's heart;
Her mourning spirit feels its soothing power,
The shades of sorrow hovering o'er her brow
Become more light, and smiling through her tears,
In all the loveliness of widow'd youth

In accents sweet her grateful heart pours forth
Its tide of thankfulness. Her Orphans dear
With sympathetic gladness, share her joy,
Cling round her near and kiss her tears away.
Such is the love the Odd-Fellowship inspires,
That naught but death itself can subdue
It's glowing warmth, or snap the bond that binds
In union sweet, that vast fraternity
Where withering sickness wastes and death destroys,
Where Widows weep and helpless Orphan's moan,
Its philanthropic power is seen, is felt
And thousands own, with gratitude untold
The value of boon. 'Tis not confined
Within the bounds of England's far domain:
It ranges wide, extending wider still,
Traversing deserts drear and oceans vast
Cementing man to man, enkindling light
And warmth, and all the joys of social bliss;
Thus smoothing o'er the chequered path of life,
Chasing the gloom which surrounds the anguished brow
And shedding on the lonely widow'd heart
The sunny rays of competence and joy.

All hail! ye happy philanthropist band!
While musing on the mighty power you wield,
To soothe the griefs of life's precarious hour
The spirit glows with sympathetic warmth,
Invades the choicest blessings on your cause
And fondly hopes the Order e'er may prove,
The Widow's solace and the Orphan's friend.

Wells Journal, April 1854

A PATRIOTIC SONG

For the warriors I plead, and hope not in vain,
Fast leaving Old England and crossing the main,
To put forth their might in the soul-stirring war,
Now moving all hearts 'gainst the Russian Czar:
And while they are bending the Muscovite low,
Ye kind hearts of Britain! Your sympathy shew;
And let the lone wives they have left in the rear,
Your tender regard and warm sympathies share.

The flag of Old England waves high on the sea
The terror of tyrants, the hope of the free
Where'er it has waved in the east or the west,
The great God of Armies its presence has blessed:
And while they are fighting, fresh laurels to gain
Remember, with pity, the wounded and slain:
And let their dear families left in the rear
Your tender regard and warm sympathies share.

Wells Journal, December 1856

THE ORPHAN'S TEAR

Beside an honour'd parent's bier,
The orphan stood and dropped a tear;
I saw his little bosom heave,
Watched the warm tear drop in the grave,
Heard his desiring sobs, and saw
That smiling boy with grief laid low.

Though young in years, that throbbing heart
Of human sorrow showed its part;
Though pure and lovely as the flowers
Which bloom in Spring's delightful hours,
A thrilling sense of anguish keen,
Bedimmed that rosy face serene.

A sense of pain ne'er expressed,
And ne'er, perchance, by man confessed,
The springs of sorrow broke, and then
Was seen displayed in mortal ken,
A picture shaded with the gloom
That settled round the closing tomb.

Yet griefs of early years, they say,
To youthful hopes will soon give way,
Just as the clouds at opening day
Dissolve before the morning ray;
And thy swollen eyes may yet be bright
And sparkle with intense delight.

Though 'neath the grass the mortal lies,
The spirit dwells beyond the skies,
Though passed away from scenes below,
He may perchance, thy sorrows know;
And He who called thy sire away
Can guide thee to the realms of day.

'Tis he that for the orphan cares,
Calms his fears and dries his tears,
Sends holy spirits down to pour,
The balm of hope in sorrow's hour,
To hover round thy path, and teach,
Thee how thy Father's home to reach.

Then fix thy tearful eye above,
And taste, in youth, thy Maker's love,
Nor e'er forget thy parent's prayer
For thee, the burden of his care,
Breath'd with his latest, deepest sigh,
That Heaven would bless thy destiny.

Wells Journal, April 1857

LINES ON A BEAUTIFUL SWAN,
BARBAROUSLY BEATEN TO DEATH IN THE PALACE MOAT[5]

No more upon the water clear
Wilt thou sweet bird, thy form display,
Nor to the slippery margin steer,
To take the offered crumb away;
Nor e'er again, with instinct rare,
Thy daily wants and wishes tell,
Making the wondering gazers stare,
By striking out thy dinner bell.

No more beneath the shady trees,
Wilt thou unfold thy snowy wing,
And glide along with graceful ease,
To beautify the spot, poor thing!
No more around the turrets grey,
Wilt thou thy morning's circuit take,
Nor fold thy wing at close of day,
Upon the bosom of the lake.

Wells Journal, June 1858

---

[5] In the *Wells Journal* of June 1858 an article appeared regarding the death of one of the palace swans: "Last week some evil-disposed person or persons cruelly beat one of the swans on the moat and the bird has since died. What could have actuated the perpetration of such a wicked act? It is too difficult to conceive. A reward of 2 guineas is offered by the Lord Bishop, the owner of the birds, for the apprehension and conviction of the offender and we sincerely trust the scoundrel or scoundrels will not long evade detection as this is not the first act of cruelty that has been committed upon the swans on the moat which surrounds the palace".

A SUMMER EVENING THOUGHT

E're scarce the lingering light of day
Has faded from the earth away,
The ruddy morn reveals Sol's eye,
Illuming all the Eastern sky,
Pouring his brightness o'er the earth,
Giving the buds and flowers birth,
And restless man another day
To trifle, like the last away.

Like Sol, declining in the West,
The righteous path to glorious rest;
Again they rise, and their glad eyes
Survey the realms beyond the skies;
And ere their light has died away
They taste the joys of endless day:
One hour, they look, their last on earth,
The next, in Heaven record their birth!

Bath Chronicle, July 1858

AMONG THE SHEAVES

I'll tune my lyre among the sheaves today,
And joy shall be the burden of the strain,
The freshening breeze shall waft it o'er the plain,
And wrinkled care shall laugh his lines away!
While sturdy rustics rear the golden mows,
While wreaths of corn we'll deck the gleaner's brows,
And make the sun-burnt beauties smile again;
With Autumn's flowers we'll trim the loaded wain,
And poor old Dobbin, too, shall wear a crown
Of scarlet berries gathered on the down.
The music of the rustling sheaves shall thrill
Each grateful heart, and make the homestead ring,
And bustling, red-faced, dames, with voices shrill,
Shall sip the pure home-brewed, and dance and sing.

Wells Journal, October 1858

ONWARDS

The opening dawn the knell has rung
Of drowsy sloth upon his bed,
The thrush its morning hymn has sung,
And all the shades of night are fled;
Fair Nature stretches forth her hand,
And lures us on with whispers sweet,
To join the thinkers of our land
And mingle with the good and great.

Then let us sow the precious seeds
That bloom and blossom into fame,
And by a roll of glorious deeds
Earn for ourselves a noble name,
Outstrip our sires in all that's good
And true, that in their history gleams,
And brush aside that lazy brood
Into the hazy land of dreams.

With purpose firm and strong, we'll try
To earn ourselves a noble name,
Aye, daily rise toward the sky,
And put the drones of earth to shame;
Triumphing o'er the toil and strife
That wear the mind and muscle down,
Resign at last our useful life,
To don the noble worker's crown.

Wells Journal, 1859

THE OPENING OF THE RAILWAY TO WELLS

The steam horse pants along the road
Where yesterday the daisies grew,
And hurries through the vale its load
Of merchandise both old and new,
The silence of our drowsy town,
Is broken by its whistle shrill
And some look up and some look down
As hopes or fears their bosoms thrill.

Where're the steam horse bounds along,
Annihilating time and space,
A stream of light, both clear and strong,
Upon its shimmering track we trace,
And every puff that dies away,
Its snowy columns to the skies,
Proclaims aloud a brighter day
Is dawning on our destinies.

Where're it tears the rugged earth,
Or o'er its level surface flies,
A shout ascends from every hearth
And fairy prospects charm the eyes,
The music of its march is heard
From town to town across our isle
And progress is the matchless word,
That makes the brow of labour smile.

Old Wells and Glaston now can shake,
Each other warmly by the hand,
And friendly words and greetings make
And shine conspicuous in the land.
And strangers from afar will stroll,
Admiring through our streets again,
Or promenade the fir cloth'd knoll
And view the beauties of the plain.

The smoke bound toiler now can live,
Away from dust, and care and strife
And picnic 'neath the open sky
And taste the joys of country life;
Can in the morn his cottage leave
Ere scarce the lark is on the wing
And sport beneath the briny wave,
And to the winds his sorrows fling.

And commerce, too, will wend her way
Towards our opened gates again,
And all her varied wares display,
And captivate with tales of gain;
And trade in all its vigour spring,
To life, beneath her genial ray,
And all her untold pleasures bring,
To usher in a brighter day.

Wells Journal, February 1859

KINDNESS

There's something in a friendly tone
That gushes from a feeling breast,
That startles Care upon his throne,
And soothes the troubled heart to rest.
Aye, sweeter than the flowers of spring,
Or summer's ever-gladdening ray,
Its music through the soul will ring,
And charm the leaden hours away.

The magic of its potent spell
Is felt in every humble hearth;
And he who would its value tell,
Or rightly estimate its worth
Must battle with the deadly strife
That wears and tears the spirit down,
And every step he takes in life,
Be thwarted by a blighting frown.

The blessed sun may brightly shine,
And Heaven upon our efforts smile,
And health and vigour both combine
To make us happy all the while;
Yet, what is life without a friend
A kindred spirit to our own
To soothe, to guide, perchance defend,
And cheer us with a loving tone?

Shepton Mallet Journal, January 1860

MUSINGS IN THE MEADOWS

The day was cloudy, yet the breeze
Came softly o'er the Southern hills,
Disporting round the budding trees,
    And playing with the daffodils;
    When I and Mary strolled along,
Well-pleased to tread the emerald sod,
    To listen to the blackbird's song,
    And see new life in every clod.

Where're we roved, some token fair
Of coming spring begemmed the scene,
    And ever on the pathways bare,
    The daisy struggled to be seen;
The rustling woods were getting gay,
With buds and blossoms just in sight,
    And golden cups along the way,
We hailed and gathered with delight.

Sweet violets, with their purple eyes,
    Were coyly peeping here and there,
Like modest worth, destined to rise,
    And revel in a brighter sphere;
    Along the lane, primroses pale,
    Unveiled their glories to the eye,
And song-birds all across the vale,
Poured forth their spring-tide melody.

We need not roam to distant lands,
For smiling fields and lovely flowers,
    Without the labour of our hands,
They come to gild our leisure hours;
They come to lure us form the din,
The smoke, the bustle and the strife,
    Which hem us city mortals in,
    To taste the charms of rural life.

Adown the flowery-margined lane,
And o'er the meadows green and gay,
    Oh! Mary we will walk again,
And spend the hours of closing day;
    That cluster round the city fair,
    And linger near the hazel copse,
And gather flowers and fancies there.

Who does not love the charming Spring?
She comes with blessings on her wings;
Again our native warblers sing,
While every nook with gladness rings.
The swallow floats adown the lane,
Or round my old straw cottage flies;
The martin claims her nest again,
And trims it with an artist's eyes.

The woods are vocal with sweet sounds,
The rills are sparkling with delight,
The farmer saunters o'er his grounds,
And care sits on his bosom light;
While round his team the wagtails play,
And squirrels in the hedges leap,
The merry ploughman hums his lay,
Or whistles o'er the furrows deep.

Old *Pleasant* doffs her Winter's coat,
And dons her sleek and silvery grey,
And in the meadows near the moat,
Enjoys her Sabbath holiday;
Ungroomed, unfettered, gay and free,
She rolls and feeds, and shakes her mane,
Oft prancing round the brave oak tree,
Or trotting down the primrose lane.

See, yonder on the sweet hawthorn,
The thrush is piping to his mate;
The milkmaid, rosy as the morn,
Is loitering near the meadow gate;
And when her lover brings the cows,
Her loving heart throbs with delight,
For faith assures her all his vows
Will be fulfilled with honour bright.

Talk not to me of city life,
I'm sick of all its boasted light,
Its mock refinement and its strife,
Its genteel vices black as night;
My weary spirit, vexed and tried,
Hies to some quiet, hill-side nook,
To feast upon the landscape wide,
And study Nature's glorious book.

Wells Journal, April 1860

SUMMER

How glorious is the Summer time
All-blooming, beautiful and grand!
Heaven's smile beams brightly on our clime,
And Beauty's pencil paints the land;
Luxuriance clothes the landscape green,
And Plenty dances on the plain;
We gaze with rapture on the scene,
And linger o'er the fields of grain.

And, oh, how sweet the evening hours!
The fragrance of the new-mown hay
The odour of the dew-gemmed flowers
The soft and tranquil twilight grey
Then with the spirit seem to blend,
Diffusing all its essence sweet,
Making the soul in homage bend,
Low at the Lord of Nature's feet.

Along the lane beside the stream
That sparkles near the hillock's side,
Where daisies shine, and roses gleam,
How sweet to stroll at eventide,
To leave awhile the bustling town,
With all its sights and sins behind,
To breathe the breeze upon the down,
And freshen up the jaded mind.

And, midst the hush and calm serene,
Of Summer's balmy evening hours,
How sweet to contemplate each scene
Upon this favoured land of ours,
And breathe to Heaven the ardent prayer,
That other lands remote from this,
May sow the germs of freedom there,
And taste with us a Briton's bliss.

Wells Journal, July 1860

MY WORN OUT BARROW

Thou'rt worn out now, old Barrow!
Thou'rt worn away indeed,
And the fact I state with sorrow,
For thou wast a friend in need;
No wind or weather heeding,
We hurried o'er the town,
The worthy natives feeding
With seconds, best and brown.

An honour to thy maker,
Who made thee light and trim,
A help-mate to the baker
Who filled thee to the brim;
And a subject for thy master,
Who writes with deep regret,
For a better or a faster,
He never handled yet.

We ran together daily,
Eighteen years or more,
And served our patrons gaily;
But thy running days are o'er,
Worn thin, and softly battered,
Beneath the apple tree,
Thy fragments now are scattered,
And there's an end of thee.

I've watched thee like a lover,
On bustling market days,
And written on thy cover,
In quiet lanes and ways,
Some verses grave and funny,
And hummed a merry strain,
While fancies sweet as honey
Were flitting through my brain.

Oh! eighteen years a striving
With the muscle and the brain,
And round the city driving,
In the sunshine and the rain;
For ever wearing, tearing,
At the oven or the barrow,
The daily burden bearing,
Hoping for a better morrow.

Aye, eighteen years a pushing,
With the toil-drops on my brow,
Poetic breathings gushing,
Treasured in memory now;
And thoughts sometimes depressing,
Which were banished and forgot,
And business matters pressing,
To complete my happy lot.

A baker's life is trying,
Watching, working, night and day,
But what's the use of sighing,
Work is better far than play;
It keeps the mind from rusting
Drives unpleasant thoughts away,
And, in heaven's goodness trusting,
Keeps us happy all the day.

'Tis not the constant toiling,
The motion of the limbs,
The face and fingers soiling;
The mental vision dims;
'Tis the needless hurry scurry,
The envy and the strife,
That ceaseless spirit worry,
That saps the springs of life.

So, with a bran new Barrow,
Kind providence permitting,
We'll start again tomorrow,
And round the town be flitting;
Like a bee among the flowers,
Or the ants upon the hill,
Making much of summer hours,
Be a cheerful toiler still.

Wells Journal, August 1860

A REVERIE[6]

Merry maids in days gone by ,
  Have sweetly smiled on me,
And at times perchance, a sigh
  Has shadowed o'er my glee,
Rich in beauty, yet richer still,
  In moral worth were some
Young and charming at the rill,
  That sparkles near my home.
Lively as the linnet's song -,
  The sweetest of the sweet,
Engaging Mary tripped along,
  The Rustic Bard to greet!
With her I gathered daisies,
  And heard the thrushes sing,
Indeed, we mingled praises,
  To nature's glorious King,
Strolling thro' flowery masses ,
  Or resting by the spring.
Worshipp'd by us both the wreath,
  Of spring, - the buds of May,
Every flower that gemmed the heath
  Or blossomed on the spray.
Lonely nooks and lovely dells
  Our feet together pressed,
Lightsome as the merry bells
  Fair Flora we caressed,
Sweetly breath'd our fond farewells
  On nature's emerald breast,
And fancied we were blest.

Wells Journal, December 1860

---

[6] Catcott never married but found young love with Mary Ann Lewis of Wells. 'A Reverie,' 'Blighted Hopes,'
'To Mary upon Receiving her Photograph,' 'Mary Ann's Grave,' and 'To Mary' tell the story of their
relationship.

MY SWEET HAWTHORN

Neath poplars high, beside a stream,
A sweet hawthorn, my present theme,
For years its leaves and berries bore,
And shaded o'er my cottage door.
'Twas planted by my honoured sire,
Who found it growing near the briar,
And moved it thence, with care and toil,
To flourish in a better soil.
In my young days I used to play
Around it's stem at close of day;
And hours, beneath its blossom fair,
I've spent in meditation there.
In summer time 'twas sweet to sit,
And read, and think, as I thought fit;
To breathe awhile the scented breeze,
Whist sitting 'neath its shade at ease;
To view the purling streamlet flow,
And watch the swallow come and go;
Observe the robin plume its wing,
And hear the cheerful blackbird sing;
And in the smiling month of May,
Admire and pluck its blossoms gay.
How charming too, its foliage green,
With sunlight streaming down between,
And zephyrs stealing through each bough,
Disporting round my weary brow!
And then how sweet at days decline,
To hear the lowing of the kine;
To see the rosy milkmaid come,
And milk her cows and then go home;
To watch the bat flit here and there,
And hear the sheep-bell tinkling near;
To mark the labourer wend his way,
All scented o'er the new-mown hay;
To hear the village bells afar,
And watch the brightening evening star
With beauty twinkling in the west,
At Luna in her silvery vest.

Sweet moments these, at evening's close,
Amidst the hush of calm repose,
To feel the deathless spirit rise,
Unlocked toward its native skies;
Forgetting all the things of earth,
To ponder on its untold worth!
Yes, these were hours to me most dear,
Hours precious, undisturbed by care;
Sweet hours! Which I shall ne'er forget
For memory lingers round them yet.

When summer's lengthy days were o'er,
And leaves and blossoms charmed no more,
Red berries then, in close array,
Were thickly clustered on each spray,
Tempting the blackbird and the thrush
To settle on the fruitful bush,
And revel unmolested there,
'Midst winter's storms and frosts severe.

But thou, sweet bush! Wilt bloom no more,
Thy shadow's gone, thy days are o'er,
And I no more shall sit and think
'Neath thee, upon the rivers brink;
Yet no rude blast, by heaven's command,
Swept thee off the fertile land:
The axe, which should have laid the poplars low,
Gave thee, sad thought, thy last, thy fatal blow.

Wells Journal, May 1862

EVENING MUSING

On Sabbath evenings calm and lone,
When I sit musing by the fire,
And feelings of a purer tone
The breast with tender thoughts inspire,
How oft before my mental eye,
My Mary's face and form appears
And days of yore, long since swept by,
An air of chastened freshness wears.

Remembered still each lovely spot,
Each walk among the summer flowers,
The breezy down, the shady grot
Where we beguiled the evening hours.
How dear to us each rural scene,
The streamlet murmuring through the vale,
The lambkins on the daisied green,
The merry warblers in the dale!

Each sight and sound that seemed to thrill
Our bosoms with supreme delight;
And in the dell or on the hill,
'Twas ever sunny, warm and bright.
Oh! that those lowering clouds which cast
Their shadows on my pathway now
Would burst, and sunshine like the past
Illume again my careworn brow.

Wells Journal, February 1863

A SUNNY MEMORY

One April morn I limped away,
For I could scarcely toddle,
I never shall forget the day,
While I've a living noddle.
The railway bell was ringing loud,
The panting engine whistled shrill,
And so I joined the travelling crowd,
And down I ran to Richmond Hill.[7]

Down through the meadows, green and gay,
With merry hearts we hied along
With men and maids I laughed that day,
And carolled to the engine's song.
On, on we went, the dust did fly
We oft admired the driver's skill,
And rattled on right merrily,
Till we got to Richmond Hill.

The sun shone bright, the day was fine
Dame Nature's face was one sweet smile,
And everything along the line
Seemed gay without a grain of guile.
So on we sped at such a rate,
And passing meadow, mount and mill,
And stream and stile and castle gate,
Soon found ourselves on Richmond Hill.

The golden furze beside the line,
The woods, the fields, the copper mine,
The straw-thatched cot, the villa neat,
The sea-washed rock, the grassy glade,
The river deep, the shallow rill,
By turns their varied charms displayed,
As we ran on to Richmond Hill.

---

[7] This Richmond Hill is in Truro, Cornwall, which Catcott visited with his friend, John Harris. Harris, the 'Miner Poet', worked in the tin mines of the Redruth, Camborne area of Cornwall and wrote about nature, his life, and times. Catcott went to visit Harris at his home, 'Six Chimneys' at Carn Brae, and the two men, who shared a similar outlook on life, exchanged letters and verse.

The memory of that happy day
Is fixed forever in my breast,
And never will it fade away,
Till 'neath the flowers I'm laid to rest;
Whate'er may be my future lot,
Or shine, or shade, or good or ill,
I never can forget that cot
Upon the top of Richmond Hill.

Its inmates were so good and kind,
So open-hearted, homely, free,
I have them in my heart enshrined,
And ever shall thy debtor be.
I longed to find a cosy crib,
To rest my limbs and keep them still;
That hearth I found, I tell no fib,
Upon the crest of Richmond Hill.

God bless the husband and the wife,
Their lusty sons and daughters too,
And all along their path of life,
The roses of contentment strew!
Down form the skies may blessings flow,
Refreshing as a Cornish rill,
And may they ne'er one sorrow know
At No. One on Richmond Hill!

Wells Journal, April 1863

OLD ENGLAND

Old England! 'tis a glorious land,
The home of peace and liberty!
The trembling slave that treads her strand,
Shakes off his chains and revels free,
While round her shores the waters play,
And bear their golden freights along,
And castles grand and churches grey,
Combine to make her bulwarks strong.

Rich meadows decked with flowers of gold,
In all their summer glories shine,
And scenes of beauty, yet unrolled,
Adorn my father's land and mine.
For ever sparkling as it flows
The merry brooklet glides along
Where blooms the daisy and the rose,
And Mary sings her evening song.

And nestling 'midst her mist crowned hills,
Sweet vales in dream-like beauty smile
While love the air with music fills
And calm contentment reigns the while
In rich profusion o'er the land
And angels guard our precious stores
Secure from every hostile hand.

And scattered o'er her hills and dells,
The hardy sons of toil we see,
Who love their dear old Sabbath bell
And worship at their altars free;
And warriors brave and statesmen wise
And Heaven taught Bards and patriots pure,
And men of mind in every size,
Abound to make her fame endure.

Long may we prize our Island home,
Thy blessed birth-land of the free,
Where wanderers from afar may come,
And breathe the air of liberty.
Still may her flowers untrampled spring,
Her harvests wave, her cities rise;
And yet, till time shall fold his wing,
Remain earth's loveliest paradise.

Wells Journal, April 1863

THE OLD GREY MARE

Beneath the verdant sod,
Where golden cowslips nod,
And ever-blooming daisies grow,
Old *Pleasant* lies at last,
Her days of labour past,
Reposing in the shade below.

Upon the meadow's brow,
Beside the old hay mow,
Just where the fragrant hawthorn's bloom,
Where, sheltered from the blast,
The primrose opens fast,
We closed, with tears, the old mare's tomb.

Let none her bones molest,
Now settled down to rest,
Far from the hum of city strife,
Where careworn mortals fret,
And hug the gold they get,
To end in gloom a gloomy life.

She freely did her part,
In wagon, plough, or cart,
For more than seven-and-twenty years;
And never from a colt,
Was known to kick or bolt,
Though cannons thundered in her ears!

Without a bit of vice,
She looked so plump and nice,
And stepped so steady and so sure,
That did it rain, or snow;
Or freeze, or thaw, or blow,
She'd bring you safely o'er the moor.

Without a single oat,
She wore a glossy coat
In Summer and in Winter too;
When young, in life's heyday,
'Twas what is termed iron grey,
But now 'twas of a lighter hue.

That coat her Maker wove,
In His great loom above,
Was never dressed by jockey rules,
Noe clipped, when wanted most
In Winter's biting frost,
To please the whims of modern fools.

We did not heed the tale,
That cutting off her tail
Would tend to make her back the stronger;
And so we deemed it wise
To let it sweep the flies,
And grow till it would grow no longer.

She was a noble mare!
She stood the wear and tear
Of years upon the Queen's highway;
She knew her daily rounds,
She loved her feeding grounds,
And thousands loved the poor Old Grey.

One resting day in seven
The Sabbath blessed by Heaven,
She always claimed and always had;
And on that glorious day,
Kept her high holiday,
And galloped o'er the meadows glad.

Those cunning, canting men,
We meet with now and then,
Who prate so much about the soul;
And give their beasts no rest
Upon the day God blessed,
Look very dim on Reason's scroll.

And could we make them look,
Into the Holy Book,
They'd see engraved on Sinai's crest,
In lines that burn and blaze,
"Observe my Sabbath days,
And give your *weary* cattle rest."

How oft upon the road,
We see the tipsy load
Of Sunday-tripping lads and lasses,
With curses on the lip,
Using the slashing whip,
And shocking every one that passes!

But I can say with pride,
Our dear old *Pleasant's* hide
Had ne'er a Sabbath mark upon it;
She worked her six days well,
Better than I can tell,
She knew the seventh, and rested on it.

No guide did she require,
To lead her through the mire,
Or show her who our patrons were;
She knew the homes of all,
Where she was wont to call,
And always stopped, and waited there.

No more upon the road,
She'll draw the steaming load
Of "quarterns" from the oven hot;
Nor climb the hills again,
Nor trot along the plain,
Nor stop before the poor man's cot.

Two years and rather more,
After her toils were o'er,
She rambled o'er the meadows free,
Cropping the herbage green,
Gemming the rural scene,
Breathing the air of liberty.

So now released from toil,
She's mingling with the soil;
And may the cowslips brighter bloom,
The daisies thicker spring,
And violets ever fling
Their fragrance round old *Pleasant's* tomb!

Shepton Mallet Journal, May 1863

39

THE DESERTED BRIDE

T'was after she became a bride,
I first beheld her sunny face;
She was of village maids the pride
The rosy glory of the place.
She was indeed, a charming thing
And e'er was ushered into birth
Far sweeter than the flowers of Spring
A gem beside the cottage hearth.

Reared far away beyond the din
And clamour of the sin-stained town,
Where cottages were scattered thin
Along the margin of the down;
Where flower-robed orchards charmed the eye,
And roses wild perfumed the lane;
Where sun-browned lovers breathed the sigh,
And frolicked round the harvest wain.

There, in that sweet sequestered spot,
Dawned the bright morning of her days,
And there she trimmed her father's cot,
And studied all his whims and ways;
There, like a flower, with dewdrops hung,
She bloomed beneath affection's sun,
And to her sire she fondly clung.
And cheered him when his toil was done.

There, too, she heard the truths sublime,
Destined to make the spirits shine
Beyond the boundary line of time,
Where all is glorious and divine;
And, there the heaven-hued path of light,
With firm, unwavering steps she trod,
And treasured up those precepts bright,
Which lead away to Heaven and God.

A tear bedimmed her father's eye,
The morn he lost his priceless flower,
She crossed the threshold with a sigh,
    And left for aye her native bower;
    Then to the town she hied away,
        Her happy lover by her side,
The song-bird trilled his sweetest lay
And carolled o'er the new-made bride.

But soon the dream of her young life,
That dream which only maidens dream,
Was shrouded o'er with care and strife,
    And hope withdrew his golden beam;
    Her madcap spouse her home upset,
        The demon drink inflamed his brain,
She made with tears her pillows wet,
And he proved false and crossed the main.

    But where he is, she cannot tell;
This much she knows, and nothing more,
    He crossed the ocean safe and well,
        And landed on a foreign shore;
        One note he sent, but never came
            Again his loving bride to own,
    But left her, with a shattered frame,
        To battle with the world alone.

    Some traces of her early grief
    Still seem to linger round her brow;
        But yet, 'tis my sincere belief,
    Her heart is somewhat lighter now;
Foe sheltered, soothed, and cheered by those
        Who try to estimate her worth,
    She more and more her goodness shows
        And smiles beside the poet's hearth.

Shepton Mallet Journal, June 1863

THE MERRY REAPERS

The evening breeze is bringing
Music from the fields of grain,
The harvesters are singing
Their sweet harvest hymn again;
The rising moon is shining
Brightly on the cotters hearth,
And the reapers in the *Tyning*
Are the happiest men on earth.

The last sheaf has been taken
Safely to the golden mow,
And matchless ale and bacon
Crown the labours of the plough;
While loosened tongues are telling
Laughing tales upon the green,
And grateful hearts are swelling
With emotion at the scene.

The reapers' hearts are warming
With the spirit-stirring ale,
And the gleaners, young and charming,
Are dancing in the dale.
A ray of hope is springing
In the breast of man and boy,
And the homestead is ringing
With the fullness of their joy.

And there's a holy feeling
Which pen cannot express,
In silent rapture stealing,
A gush of thankfulness,
O'er that delighted party;
And we linger on the plain
Till their carols loud and hearty,
Make the welkin ring again.

The God of Peace is smiling
From His throne above the sky,
And plenty for the toiling
Million, meets the gladdened eye;
Then dry your tears, ye weepers,
Let your voices loud and strong,
Commingle with the reapers
In their merry harvest song.

Wells Journal, September 1863

TO MY NEPHEW WILLIAM HENRY CATCOTT
IN THE ARMY OF THE POTOMAC

William! Wherever thou mayest be,
While fighting with the brave and free,
May holy angels ever spread
Their sheltering wings around thy head!
And should thy future lot be cast
'Midst forests dense, or prairies vast
Along the silvery river's side,
Or on the ocean's swelling tide;
Or crossing plains, or climbing hills,
When summer warms, or winter chills,
When flowery spring perfumes the fields,
Or autumn her rich harvest yields,
In every time and every place,
Whilt running o'er thy destined race,
May heaven's own sweet approving smile,
Beam brightly on thee all the while!
May every ball and cannon shot
Fly o'er thy head and harm thee not,
And no war-weapon of the foe
E'er cause thy gentle blood to flow!
May God in mercy end the strife,
The awful sacrifice of life,
And crown with glorious victory
The army of the brave and free.
Safe to thy father's hearth again,
Without a scar or moral stain,
Mayest thou in triumph soon return,
To soothe the hearts that o'er thee yearn,
Thy mother and thy sister dear;
To greet thy father with a cheer,
A thrilling cheer of grateful joy,
And prove thyself a noble boy.

Wells Journal, October 1863

THE DAISY ON MY MOTHER'S GRAVE

We buried her, 'twas in the early spring,
Beneath the sod. A daisy here and there,
Bedecked the green around the house of prayer,
And now when'er I see that smiling thing,
My thoughts revert to her and that event,
As if it were from heaven a messenger sent,
To stamp the past more deeply on my breast.
Sweet flower! I loved thee in my boyish days
And thought thee more lovely than the rest,
Though rudely crushed upon the lone pathways.
But since that saddening time, thou art more dear,
And oft at eve I've plucked thee with a tear,
And musing fondly on the spirit's rest,
With eager hands have bound thee to my breast.

Wells Journal, November 1863

FRIENDSHIP
(A True Story)

I thought I had a noble friend,
A loving, true and trusty one,
Whose merry heart beat time with mine,
And all its faith and favour won;
He seemed all truth and honour bright,
Free, firm and faithful in my eyes
The model of a perfect man,
As pure and open as the skies.

Year after year, our joys and cares,
Our wishes, wants and other things,
We poured into each other's ears,
With all the trust that friendship brings;
And every hope and every fear
That daily trembled in our breast,
Became at eventide our theme,
Before we nestled down to rest.

We climbed the hills and trod the dales
That beautify our native isle,
And roses wild and sweet we plucked
Beneath the Sabbath evening's smile;
We paced with lightsome step the fields
Fresh shorn, where fragrant hay was made,
And mused beside the sparkling stream,
And rested 'neath the willow's shade.

Together side by side we went,
Till fate decreed that we should part;
He sailed across the Western sea,
And left me with a throbbing heart;
But still his kind epistles came,
And still my prayers and wishes went
To sooth him in the far-off West,
And cheering words to me he sent.

Ten years thus swiftly passed away,
When I beheld his form again,
I warmly pressed the offered hand,
While gladness danced in every vein;
The best of welcomes I could give,
I proudly on my friend bestowed,
Placed bed and board at his command,
And every kind attention showed.

But what a change these years had wrought!
For when he left I missed a friend
The best, perhaps, I ever knew,
And thought our friendship n'er would end;
'Tis painful to record the fact,
I found him now a different man,
A grasping, selfish, mean "Yankee"
A flint, a perfect Jonathan!

There must, I'm sure, be something wrong
In that slave-torturing, blood stained land,
To blight like this the genial soul,
And sever friendship's sacred band;
My aching heart swells with the thought,
That teachings and examples vile,
The noblest natures sometimes spoil,
And sink them deep in guilt and guile.

Wells Journal, November 1863

46

IN MEMORIUM

Two pilgrim's on life's rugged road
With loving hearts I knew,
Led by their heavenly Father's hand,
In virtue daily grew;
For nearly threescore years they lived,
And loved from year to year;
In shine and shadow still the same,
Still to each other dear.

The glorious sun one Summer eve,
Went down in golden light,
To shine upon the western wave
And chase the gloom of night:
The birds trilled soft their vespers sweet,
The moon concealed her face
Behind the fleecy clouds that sailed
Along in star-lit space.

Anon, the bell with thrilling power,
The drowsy sleeper woke,
By booming out the midnight hour,
With slow and solemn stroke!
In that dark hour how hard to part,
Two hearts united long!
Yet heaven decrees, and Death lays low
The weakly and the strong.

The tender husband, weeping sees
The partner of his life,
To the green grave-yard borne along,
And mourns a loving wife;
And in that ne'er forgotten spot
The cloister walls surround,
The lonely mourner walks and weeps,
Beside her hallowed mound.

Remembers how her virtues shone,
And brightened up his hearth,
And how she strove to make his home,
The sweetest place on earth;
And then he looks beyond the clouds
Toward the spirit-land,
And hopes one day to meet her there,
Among the ransomed band.

Wells Journal, December 1863

LINES TO THE MEMORY OF KIT,
WHO WAS KILLED BY A GREYHOUND, 7TH OCTOBER 1847

I can't forget thee Kit! I try,
But still the tear bedims my eye;
Thy mangled form, besmeared with gore,
Exuding from each opening sore,
Before my mental vision lies,
While saddening thoughts each moment rise,
And round my restless spirit cling;
And memory too, that potent thing,
Lashes afresh my wounded breast,
And makes me vainly wish for rest.

I can't forget thee Kit! for thou
On memory's scroll art written now,
And all thy frolics from thy birth,
And all thy antics on the hearth,
Thy cheery purring, and thy pranks
Upon the garden walks and banks,
And all thy loving, winsome ways,
As pleasing as a poet's lays,
Have left their impress on my brain,
And kindled up a mournful strain.

Thou wast indeed, a bosom friend,
A close companion to the end;
Upon my shoulder thou would'st spring,
And make my ears with music ring,
Cling to my breast and nestle there,
Beguiling oft the hours of care,
And through nights cold and dreary,
While I've been watching weary,
And passed alone the midnight hour,
Oh! then I've felt thy soothing power,
Experienced all thy fondness rare,
And quite forgot my load of care.

Unchanged through every changing scene,
No vices marked thy life serene,
No hearts by thee with pain were wrung,
No lies e'er travelled from thy tongue,
No malice gleamed from thy bright eye,
No envy soiled thy purity,
No anger burned within thy breast,
No cruel deeds disturbed thy rest,
No treacherous smile e'er marred thy face,
No guile in thee e'er found a place,
No sickening pride e'er turned thy brain,
Or made thee of thy beauty vain.

The first to rush across the floor,
And meet me at my cottage door,
When twilight came and closed the day,
And cheer me with thy evening lay.
And to thy watchful ear alone
My weary, homeward step was known,
And constant as the evening came,
Thy earnest greeting was the same;
The same when glorious Summer smiled,
As when the icy blast howled wild,
The same in Autumn and in Spring,
A happy and a playful thing.

When from my couch I early rose,
And paid my visit to the troughs,
I can't a single instance mind,
When thou hast lingered far behind;
Thy welcome cry was always heard,
And thy caress was n'er deferred.
Thy fondness too, was all sincere,
Unlike the mask which mortals wear,
Too oft put on the heart to tear.
No sordid motive prompted thee,
Nor soiled thy Nature's purity.
I loved thee Kit, for thou to me
Was all that treacherous man should be,
And long 'twill be ere I shall find,
A friend so true amongst mankind.

Wells Journal, March 1864

LIZZIE'S PATHETIC APPEAL TO HARRY

There's lots of teasing men about
I've seen a pretty many,
Some tall, some thin and others stout
And some not worth a penny;
But there is one whose voice I know,
Down where the puffers tarry,
Beats all the lot both high and low,
My own, my happy Harry.

Don't dearest go away just yet,
Don't leave the railway station
And make my cheeks with tear-drops wet,
By rambling o'er the nation;
I only wish I knew the worst,
I'm nearly drowned in sorrow;
I'm pretty sure my heart will burst,
If he goes off tomorrow.

I'm sure he'd better stay with me,
And watch the steam horse racing;
But if he goes beyond the sea,
His shadow I'll be chasing.
Oh! don't for goodness sake leave Wells,
And make my heart so sorry,
We may yet hear the merry bells
Ringing for me and Harry.

Wells Journal, April 1864

TO A PRIMROSE,
BROUGHT FROM THE GARDEN OF THE CORNISH POET

Up in the light of sunny day,
I saw thee in the April-bloom,
And brought thee form thy home away
To shed for me thy sweet perfume,
And didst thou know how much I prize
Thee, O, thou lovely Cornish gem!
Thou would'st not close they yellow eyes,
Nor droop so on thy tiny stem.

Beside the ivied, moss-crowned wall,
I've set thee in the border neat,
And leaflets where the sunbeam's fall,
I've strewed, to shadow thee, my sweet!
Look up, my pride! My hearts delight!
And greet me with thy genial smile,
And warm my heart, and charm my sight,
And beautify my bower a-while.

Upon the crest of Camborne-hill,
To deck the poet's native bower,
Nature decreed it in her will,
Thou should'st unfold thy virgin flower;
And there the minstrel mused beside
Thee, in the star-lit evening hours,
And sometimes sang, but oftener sighed,
And dropped a tear among'st the flowers.

Transplanted thence into the town,
To deck the poet's garden there,
The Spring-tide glory of the down
Bloomed brightly 'neath his watchful care;
And with its blossoms fancies came,
And flitted through and through his brain,
Till all the scenes in life's young dream
Came dancing up his path again.

And a memento dear to me,
Thou smiling Angel of the dells!
For ever henceforth thou wilt be,
While I sojourn in dear old Wells;
For every time I pass thee by,
Will fancy wander to the spot
Where, 'neath the loving poet's eye,
Thy blossoms graced his garden plot.

And I shall see within his bower,
His rose-buds dear, his darling Jane
And think upon them every hour,
And long to press their hands again;
And sun-lit pictures, rich and rare,
Of pleasures crowding round his hearth,
Will rise before my vision clear,
And gem that hallowed spot of earth.

Wells Journal, April 1864[8]

---

[8] As two three-stanza poems, 'My Cornish Primrose' and 'Primroses from Cornwall to Wells.'

THE BOTTLE

I knew a jolly fellow, young and strong,
Whose prospects brightened as he went along,
Whose early life was like a sunny day,
With fortune smiling on him all the way;
Without a single stain upon life's page,
He passed from rosy youth the middle age;
Then gathering clouds hung lowering o'er his head,
A loving wife was numbered with the dead.
He sought the maddening bottle for relief,
And saddening was his wild career and brief.
His days and nights were in the alehouse spent,
And everything he had to ruin went;
And staggering homeward tipsy from the town,
One lovely morn in May, he tumbled down,
Just when the Sabbath bells began to chime,
And broke his neck, and perished in his prime.

Wells Journal, April 1864

MORNING

The blessed morning light,
So precious to my sight,
Is brightening up my quiet little room;
The birds upon the sprays
Pour forth their song of praise,
And fragrant flowers are shedding sweet perfume.

The milkmaid with a smile,
Is crossing yonder stile,
And leaving tracks along the dewy path;
The gentle stirring breeze
Is waking up the bees,
And they come humming o'er the mower's swath.

The sturdy toiler goes
As ruddy as the rose,
A-whistling down the winding primrose lane;
The gardener with his spade,
The butcher at his trade
Are singing o'er their morning hymns again.

The shepherd on the hill,
The miller in the mill,
The sun-browned sailor tossed upon the main;
The farmer and old Watch,
Beside the garden hatch,
Are basking in the morning light again.

The baker and the bard,
The labourer and the lord,
The blushing damsel and the sighing swain;
The sower, sowing grain,
The teamster with the wain,
Are moving in the morning light again.

The merchant in his store,
The thresher on the floor,
The city dandy with his empty brain;
The soldier in the camp,
The miner in the damp,
Are full of life in morning light again.

Singing its morning song,
The steam-horse bounds along,
And makes the valleys tremble with its lay;
On, on the giant goes,
Nor cares for friends or foes,
But hurries onward o'er its iron way.

Let sleepy sluggards bide
And turn from side to side,
On beds of down, stagnating blood and brain;
Fresh as the daisy sweet,
Let me the morning greet,
And revel in the cheering light again.

Upon the breezy down
Let me glance o'er the town,
And feast awhile upon the flowery plain;
And while I gaze, spell-bound,
Upon the fertile ground,
With gladness greet the merry morn again!

Wells Journal, July 1864

SHADED FLOWERS

We love the plants that deck the lawn,
And blossom round the cottage door
Breathing in summer's early dawn
Their mingled fragrance fresh and pure.
We lavish on them all our care,
And watch them with a lover's eyes,
Lingering o'er the colours rare,
They daily borrow from the skies.

But flowers as fair oft in the glade,
In silence rise between the weeds,
To waste their perfume in the shade,
Like humble men of gentle deeds;
Like those whose lives and mental might,
Demand our homage and our aid,
Yet, whom I fear we often slight,
And leave, half-starving, in the shade.

Amid the shades of humble birth,
The choicest gems we sometimes find,
Who, quite unconscious of their worth,
Bloom brightly in the realm of mind;
And, spite of bramble or of bough,
Nobly work out their purpose grand,
Climb bravely up life's rugged brow,
Diffusing fragrance o'er the land.

Wells Journal, September 1864

THE SOLDIER'S PRAYER

Stern duty calls, and I must leave,
Thee, charming Mary for a while,
To wrestle with the bold and brave
Defenders of my native isle;
But while I'm borne upon the tide
Towards the Czar's immense domain,
May Heaven protect thee, oh, my bride,
Till victory wafts me home again!

The loud huzzas that greet my ears,
Whilst hastening on to help the Turk,
Inspire my heart, dispel my fears,
And fit me for the glorious work.
And while we're struggling side by side,
Upon the battle's blood-stained plain,
May Heaven sustain thee, oh, my bride,
Till victory wafts me home again!

Wells Journal, September 1864

LINES SUGGESTED BY AN ADVERTISEMENT FOR A "MAID OF ALL WORK" CONTAINING THE WORDS, "NO METHODISTS NEED APPLY"[9]

"No Methodist need apply!"
What a gem in Satan's eye
Must the advertiser be!
He must needs enslave the free
He must think and none but he,
He, of creeds the umpire be!
He would chain the God-made mind,
And the soul in fetters bind.

"No Methodist need apply!"
In the name of goodness, why?
"Tis her labour thou dost need,
"Tis her hands, and not her creed.
Must she, with spirit meek,
In distant lands her living seek?
Must she knock until she faints,
In a land of liberal saints?

"No Methodist need apply!"
Can you give the reason why?
Can you in her conduct spy
Any blot that shocks the eye?
Can you in her features trace
Anything but modest grace?
Can you in her history con
Anything to frown upon?

"No Methodist need apply!"
Tell me, brother Christian, why?
Canst thou look toward the sky
And the Great Supreme defy?
Canst thou dive into her soul,
And its inmost thoughts control?
Wouldst thou crush that Pilgrim-band
In this favoured Bible-land?

---

[9] Printed in the 'Jobs Vacant' column of the *Wells Journal* on the 17 October 1864.

"No Methodist need apply!"
Were she pure as yonder sky,
Fairer than the flowers that gem,
Flora's May-day diadem
Holy as a seraph bright
In the upper realms of light,
Still the bigot's cry would be;
"No vile Methodists for me!"

"No Methodist need apply!"
Is this Christianity?
Does the bible teach you so?
Conscience promptly answers, No.
Don't you know the Golden Rule
Taught in every infant school?
Why 'tis clear as Heaven's light,
That you're sinning in its sight.

"No Methodist need apply!"
Will that Pharisaic cry
E'er be echoed in the skies?
Will the record of her sighs,
Precious in an angel's eyes,
Be forgotten when she dies?
Will the bigot, with his rod,
Drive the spirit from its God?

"No Methodist need apply!"
Will that spirit never die
That revels in a martyr's groans,
Tramples on his mangled bones,
And with gory fiend -like hand,
Strews his ashes o'er the land?
Will that spirit never die?
"NEVER" is the bigot's stern reply.

Wells Journal, 24 October 1864

TO A PRIMROSE IN THE CATHEDRAL GREEN.

Hail thou glory of the Spring!
Blooming in November drear,
Where the Summer warblers sing,
And the sparrow twitters near;
Close beside the rich man's hall,
Where the shrubs are green and gay,
Where the ivy decks the wall,
And the robin trills his lay.

Faithful herald of the spring!
Glorious gem on Winter's brow!
Cheering hearts that round thee cling,
With thy spring-tide splendour now.
Precious is thy yellow eye,
Gleaming through the mist and rain,
Brightening 'neath a frowning sky,
Shedding sweet perfume again.

Wells Journal, November 1864

SUNNY SUE'S BIRTHDAY

Sing a song for sunny Sue,
As fresh and fair as flowery May,
And greet her with a Stanza new,
Upon her coming natal day;
I'll hail her tripping down the stairs
And soothe her with a simple strain,
And make her dance upon her cares,
And smile her brightest smile again.

The music of her pattering feet
At morn or eve I long to hear,
When fondly I rush in to meet
Her stepping from the bottom stair;
Fresh as the dewy morn of Spring,
And fairer than the Summer flower;
Oh! what a lively, loving thing
To gem the rustic poet's bower.

There's gladness in her loving eye,
And sunshine in her genial smile,
And, oh! there's rapture in that sigh
Breathed from a heart devoid of guile!
More prized than jewels are the words
Dropped from her lips beneath the trees,
And sweeter than the song of birds
Born on the gentle evening breeze.

God bless my Sunny Sue! and grant
Her many bright and happy days!
And never, never, may she want
A faithful friend to sing her praise!
May every blessing Heaven can shower,
To charm and cheer her heart and hearth,
Encircle round her smiling bower,
And make her Home a blessed berth!

Wells Journal, November 1864

AN ACROSTIC ON THE EMINENT LECTURER, LINGUIST AND PHILANTHROPIST ELIHU BURRIT[10]

Enlightened herald of a glorious day
Let all earth's peopled realms thy voice obey,
Inglorious war shall then be chased away;
His gory-car no more o'er millions roll,
Unheard shall be his roar from pole to pole!

Benignant peace sweet guest of heavenly birth,
Unchecked, shall settle on the blood-stained earth,
Raise high her olive branch o'er the land and wave,
Restoring man the rights Jehovah gave,
Implanting firm the germs of concord dear,
Till fused in one celestial union here,
The nations all their Maker's stamp shall bear.

Wells Journal, December 1864

---

[10] Elihu Burrit, the 'Learned Blacksmith' was born in America in 1810. He grew up in humble circumstances and eventually became a blacksmith. He was self-educated and by the age of thirty could read in fifty languages. He was very active in the Abolitionist movement and was a promoter of world peace. President Abraham Lincoln appointed him US consul to England and Burrit travelled around the United Kingdom lecturing on the causes of abolition and peace.

CHRISTMAS

Come, Christians, clear the clouded brow!
Bring sunshine with the holly bough;
Come, gather round the blazing fire,
And strike again the Christmas lyre;
Suspend the shining mistletoe,
And let the festive bowl o'erflow.

The merry bells in yonder tower,
Are telling of the glorious hour,
When angels trilled their seraph-lay
To usher in the heaven-blessed day,
A day impearled with love and light,
With hallowed joys and memories bright.

Then, while the angry-wind god roars,
Ye generous hearts, unlock your stores,
Throw open wide the larder door
Fill to the brim the shivering poor,
And let the laps of want and woe
The burden of your bounties know!

And cluster round the bright wood fire
That warms your venerated sire,
Ye lusty sons and daughters gay,
And charm the lingering hours away,
With loving tales and love-lit eyes,
Till firmer grow the family ties.

Let smiles begin and end the day,
Let lads and lasses have their say;
Let Friendship, with her genial smile,
Reign o'er our dear old native isle,
And severed friends and families meet,
And mingle in communion sweet.

Shepton Mallet Journal, December 1864

THE VILLAGE CHURCHYARD

Can you pass the village church,
Where the sparrow loves to perch,
Where the weeping willows bloom,
Shading o'er the silent tomb,
Where the ashes of your sire
Rest beneath the pointed spire
Can you treads the sod, tear-wet,
And the hallowed spot forget?

Other thoughts may come and go,
Deeply tinged with weal or woe,
Fancy with her magic wand,
Waft you to another land;
But the memory lingers here,
O'er departed kindred dear,
Till their spirits seem to glide,
From the flowerets by our side.

Then we carry to our bowers,
Treasured thoughts of spring-tide hours,
When we rambled o'er the hills,
Gathering golden daffodils,
And expressed our fears and hopes
By the sheltering hazel copse,
While the music of the brook
Pleased us better that the book.

Scattered now those friends so dear,
Like the Autumn's leaflets sere;
Some are gone beyond the line
Where the golden nuggets shine;
Some the crowded city try,
Till they in the churchyard lie,
'Neath the daisy-spotted sod,
Guarded by their Father's God.

We may breathe the bitter sigh
For our kindred when they die,
But we brush away the tear
While we fancy they are near,
And our Maker glorify,
Growing meeter for the sky,
Thinking on the friends we love,
In their glory-home above.

Wells Journal, December 1864

STANZAS WRITTEN ON RECEIVING SOME PRIMROSES
FROM A FRIEND AT TRURO

Thanks, thanks for the flowers
From Cornwall's green bowers;
Those primroses sweet, though drooping and pale,
How they put me in mind
Of loving friends warm and kind,
And softly whisper their heart-cheering tale!

Ye beautiful flowers,
Adorning our bowers!
How rich are your hues, when fresh from the grove,
Ye come smiling and gay
From dear friends far away
Breathing of friendship and beaming with love!

Oh! ye tell of a friend
Near the famous Land's End,
Whose honoured name I shall ever revere,
Of a bright son of toil,
As e'er honoured the soil,
Of a name hallowed by Gratitude's tear.

Though the hours were but few,
That I tarried with you
Yet, t'was then, the seeds of friendship were sown
For your kindness was such,
That I then felt it much,
And now feel it more, when weary, and lone.

The attentions you paid,
And the kind things you said,
Oft make the warm tear of gratitude flow;
And the soft downy bed,
Where you pillowed my head
I shall remember wherever I go.

Oh! those slices of ham,
Relished more than roast lamb,
The eggs you so nicely fried in the pan,
And the fine flavoured tea,
You provided for me,
Make me remember the kind Cornish man.

May rich blessings in store
Cheer your hearts more and more,
While marching life's chequered pathway along!
May your dear children thrive
More and more as they strive,
Till you all reach the Saint's Home with a song!

Wells Journal, March 1865

EMILY'S BIRTHDAY

I love to sing a maiden's birthday lay,
I love the daylight and the midnight sky
I love to gaze upon the moon and stars;
When ever-changing clouds are sailing by;
I love the rippling of the pebbly brook;
I love the rolling of the restless sea,
And everything bright, beautiful and fair
But thee, best of all, sweet Emily.

I love the voice of every singing bird;
On the meadows green I love to gaze;
I love the cattle on the glorious hills,
And the glorious hills on which they graze,
I love to stroll adown the primrose lane,
I love the flowers which gem the fragrant lea,
And everything bright, beautiful and fair
But thee, best of all, sweet Emily.

I love the spring time and I dearly love
The glowing splendour which the summer brings;
I love the golden autumn and the snow
Which winter on earth's forehead softly flings,
I love the noble deeds which many have done,
I love the stirring voice of poesy,
And everything bright, beautiful and fair
But thee, best of all sweet Emily.

Wells Journal, May 1865

EMMA'S BIRTHDAY

Sweetly birds are singing,
Gladsome memories bringing,
Whilst the flowers are springing
In the greening nooks and dells,
Around the spot where Emma dwells.

Traces of good Nature
Brightening every feature
Of the lovely creature,
Delight us when we meet her,
And lovingly we greet her.

Ever, ever smiling,
Trying, trusting, toiling,
Moments dark beguiling,
Striving in this world of strife,
For a brighter, better life.

Always kind and cosy,
With her cheeks as rosy
As a Summer posy,
Fairer than the hawthorn spray,
Fragrant with its blossoms gay.

'Tis her birthday, bless her!
Sisters sweet caress her!
With Spring blossoms dress her!
Crown her, crown her beauty's queen,
On the daisy-spotted green!

Spirits bright attend her!
Guard the bud so tender!
To life's end defend her,
Guide her through this vale of sighs
To a home above the skies!

Shepton Mallet Journal, May 1865

BLIGHTED HOPES

Long years of toil have rolled away,
Since that delightful summer's day,
When in the fields we plucked the flowers;
When, with a passion pure and warm,
I idolised thy every charm,
And passed with thee my happiest hours.

Untouched by care, my heart was light,
My hopes and prospects too were bright,
And cheered by thy perennial smile,
Sweet visions rose of happy days,
Illumed by warm affection's rays,
Unshaded by a tinge of guile.

With fondness undisguised and real,
Our hearts breathed forth their simple tale,
And sweetly wiled the hours away;
And as the precious moments flew,
A glorious future seemed in view,
Advancing with the coming day.

And if a shade of sorrow stole
Into the temple of the soul,
'Twas transient as the morning air;
It passed like summer clouds away,
Leaving no token of its stay,
To dim the hopes we treasured there.

But evanescent as the ray
That gilds the spires at closing day,
Or like the fleeting meteor's gleam,
Thus streams in beauty through the sky,
The hopes we deemed to bright to die,
Were nothing but a morning dream.

For ere youth's summer days were passed,
My loving Mary breathed her last;
And left me spiritless and lone;
Since then a cloud of sadness black,
Has hovered o'er my onward track,
And almost turned my heart to stone.

My thoughts for ever brooding o'er
The days that will return no more,
Cling closely to their mournful theme;
My heart is welded to the past,
To early joys too pure to last,
And every season seems the same.

One thought alone my spirit cheers,
And somewhat lightens all its cares,
The hope that when my spirit flies
Away to yonder realms of light,
It may again with her unite,
And form a union in the skies.

Wells Journal, August 1865

WORDS OF WELCOME

Our Floral Holiday!
We must, we will be gay
We'll crowd the gates of Langhorn Park again,
And spend our golden hours
Among the God-sent flowers,
And leave our cares outside the peopled plain.

Again our brave old town,
Has donned its emerald crown,
And wreathed her brow with laurels green and gay:
While graceful mottos shine,
Beside the planed pine
And notes of gladness usher in the day.

The music of the bells
Floats softly o'er our dells
Awakening sounds and rapture far and near:
And arches green and grand,
Like smiling monarchs stand,
And words of welcome on their bosoms wear.

Above the house tops high,
Our banners charm the eye
And flutter in the balmy summer breeze,
And strains of music sweet,
Resound in every street,
And warblers trill their notes on yonder trees.

The great steam horse today,
Speeds gaily on its way
With oaken boughs and flags and roses crowned,
And, like a giant strong
Flies with its load along,
O'er rock and rill, towards our pleasure ground.

Oh! may the day be bright,
And every heart be light,
And far off strangers feel themselves at home,
Among our flowers and fruits,
Our roses and our roots,
And ne'er forget our kindness when they come.

Then let us haste away
And mingle with the gay,
And meet the old familiar faces dear,
We loved in days of yore,
Give them greeting more,
And drop on friendship's shrine a grateful tear.

Shepton Mallet Journal, August 1865

LINES ON A PICNIC PARTY AT KNOLL HILL, SHEPTON MALLET

A glorious picnic party? Bless my heart,
Close up the pent up shop, and off we'll start.
Adieu to toil, to dust and blanching care,
Here's off to breathe once more the freshening air;
To ramble o'er the verdant fields awhile,
And there the chilling cares of life beguile.
View nature's matchless beauties fresh and fair
And pay due homage to our maker there.

Oh! 'tis a treat, a blessed treat, to quit
The stifling bosom of the town, to sit
Beneath the spreading branches of some oak,
And freely breathe pure air instead of smoke,
Glance o'er the chequered landscape far and wide,
And watch the winding streamlet smoothly glide,
With murmurs soft, adorn the fertile dale,
While songsters sweet emparadise the vale.

The youths are mustering the maidens fair,
Are moving onwards anxious to be there
With joyful heart, the city walls they pass
Bound o'er the stiles and tread the new mown grass.
A shady lane at length they reach, and there
Beside the hedge they spread the choicest fare;
Meanwhile a blazing fire the kettle warms
And real Souchong appears in all its charms.

Yes 'neath the open sky they spread a feast
The novel scene to all imparts a zest
But seldom felt; the damsels active smile
The sterner sex, with words devoid of guile
Express the pleasures rare, and matrons staid
With looks of satisfaction sweet, declare
That love, and peace and joy are reigning there.

Oh! who can paint a happier scene than this?
Just glance again; see you no signs of bliss?
There on the daisied bank, the lover pours
Into the maidens ear his bosom stores
Of true and faithful love; and there the sire
Beside his spouse in holiday attire,
Devout with deep emotion, views the scene,
Delighted with the banquet on the green.

The shadows lengthen and the hearty meal
Enjoyed so much in that refreshing vale,
Is finished with a song of thankfulness.
And now each happy swain and rosy lass
The neighbouring mount ascends and soon the whole
In little groups are scattered o'er the knoll
Where Nature's beauties more extensive meet
The eye, and fill the breast with joy complete.

Far from that dear spot, the view with senses charm,
And fill the soul with feelings pure and warm;
Fair verdant fields, and flocks and waving corn
Of different kinds, its southern slopes adorn.
Down through the narrow vale a streamlet flows,
Whose murmurs scarce disturb the sweet repose,
While smoking homesteads few and far between
Impart an air of comfort to the scene.

The sun is setting and the glowing west
Now captivates them more than all the rest,
The view on every side which meets the eye,
The Mendip Hills, the golden tinted sky,
Inspire the heart with wonder, joy and praise
And in one simultaneous burst they raise
In union sweet, their tuneful voices high
In anthems to the Lord of earth and sky.

Shepton Mallet Journal, August 1865

OUR FLOWER SHOW[11]

From dell and down, now haste away
Ye merry swains and maidens gay,
And breathe perfume in Langhorne's bowers,
Amidst our wild and culture flowers;
Come see our streets with laurel's crowned,
With garlands smiling all around,
While banners wave and motto's shrine,
Beside the newly-planted pine.

Come, leave your cares and toils behind,
Relax the limbs, refresh the mind,
For young and old for high and low,
We bid the rills of pleasure flow,
Come taste out fruit, come smell our flowers,
Match, if you can, these roots of ours;
Come forth from hamlet, hive and hall,
And make our show the best of all.

Shepton Mallet Journal, August 1865

---

[11] The Shepton Mallet Flower Show was held every August at Langhorn Park. It was started in 1859 by the Shepton Mallet and East Somerset Horticultural Society and offered over £150 in prizes.

THE FLOWER SHOW

Another glorious gala day
Has brightly dawned and died away;
Then let me breathe a gladsome strain,
While fancy roves among the flowers
That bloomed to-day in Langhorn's bowers,
And flung their fragrance o'er the plain.

Oh! 'tis a day red-lettered, bright,
Rich with mementos of delight,
Which memory fondly lingers o'er;
A holiday for young and old,
Impearled with blessing manifold,
And yearly honoured more and more.

A day for every class and creed,
For every toiler, labour-freed,
For high-born Lord and Lady gay;
A sunny day of pleasures sweet,
When distant friends and families meet,
And mingle in a loving way.

The steam-horse bounds along to-day,
The brisker for the holiday;
And as he pulls and puffs along,
The echoes of his music shrill,
The hearts of toil-stained workers thrill,
And make then swell and burst with song.

We love to spend our quiet hours
Where Flora gems the rich man's bowers,
Where science aids her stars of earth;
Nor love we less the garden neat,
Gemmed with the rose and wall-flower sweet,
Which blossoms round the cotter's hearth.

But what a show of flowers and fruits,
Rich-flavoured, rare, delicious, roots,
And brilliant gens of rustic skill,
O'er-brimmed the lap of gay Langhorn!
And, Oh! 'twas such a bright-eyed morn
That thousands flocked down from mart and mill.

How gaily, too, the town was dressed
She wore a smile for every guest,
And wreathed a "Welcome" on her crest;
With firs, and flowers, and banners trimmed,
Her face with sylvan beauty beamed,
And dazzling was her festal vest!

The shades of evening close around:
Success the floral fete has crowned,
And merry men and maidens fair,
Whose weary feet had travelled miles,
Now leave the Park with joy-lit smiles,
Charmed with the gems that sparkled there.

Oh! Shepton, homely, hearty, free!
Our warmest thanks are due to thee
For spreading such a feast of flowers;
Long may thy floral enterprise
Be honoured with the brightest skies
That halo o'er this land of ours.

Shepton Mallet Journal, August 1865

THE DAISY

Close beside the old wood pile,
Daisy hailed me with its smile,
And its bright eye seemed to say;
"Happy be, the live long day:
Happy when the trees are green,
Happy when no leaf is seen,
Happy when the skies are bright,
Happy midst the shades of night,
Happy when the heavens frown,
And the chilling showers come down;
Happy in the evening hour,
When the zephyrs fan the bower;
Happy when the tempest roars,
When the boatmen ply their oars;
Happy in the budding Spring,
When the woods with music ring;
Happy when the Summer comes,
And the bee her carol hums;
Happy in the Autumn-tide,
When your wants are all supplied,
And the farmer walks along
Brimming o'er with grateful song;
Happy in the Winter time,
Battling with the frost and rime;
Happy in the snow and sleet,
Coming down on field and street;
Happy by the cosy fire,
Stringing up the shattered lyre;
Will it, will it, and you may,
Happy be the live-long day."

Let us bravely will it, then,
Act our parts like noble men,
Like the daisy upward look,
Drinking truth from heaven's book,
Mingling with the good and wise,
Till we reach the upper skies.

Shepton Mallet Journal, September 1865

HARVEST HOME

Come praise the Lord for sun and shade,
For morning dews and moistening showers,
For bending bough and rising blade,
For fertile fields and fragrant flowers:
Let praises ring from dale and down,
From pastures green, where cattle roam,
From sunny heath and smoky town,
For every gladdening Harvest Home.

A Harvest Home! Oh, what a theme
For peasant's praise or poet's lay!
Come bow before the Great Supreme,
And own to-day His sovereign sway;
He bids the seasons roll along,
Bringing rich blessings when they come,
And leave, inspiring grateful song,
And hence our happy Harvest Home.

See, clustered round the homestead now,
The golden mows of garnered gain!
The farmer wipes his sun-burnt brow,
And breathes to Heaven a grateful strain;
While gleaners gay, and reapers strong,
Hilarious to the banquet come,
And sip the ale, and swell the song
That crowns our merry Harvest Home.

Oh! Ye who dig and ye who drive,
And ye who sow and ye who mow,
And ye who strive, and ye who thrive,
Ye heirs of wealth, and sons of woe,
From furzy mount, and flowery dell,
From castle, court and cottages come,
And let your swelling anthem tell
Your gladness for a Harvest Home.

Come dress the church, and trim the lawn,
And spread the feast among the flowers,
And let the gathering be the dawn
Of better days and brighter hours;
And while the bells the tidings tell,
Muse on more lasting joys to come,
When to earth's scenes we bid farewell,
And join an angels' Harvest Home.

Wells Journal, September 1865

THE THATCHER'S DAUGHTER[12]

'Twas when the nuts were getting brown,
  On sunny slopes and sheltered places,
And when the sun was shining down
  Upon the reapers backs and faces,
A bonny blue-eyed maid was born,
  Of parents kind, though poor and lowly;
Her father thatched the farmer's corn;
  Her mother was a matron holy.

They named their rosebud, 'lizabeth,
  Her nursing deemed a pleasing duty,
And bonny Bessy grew beneath
  Their care into a rosy beauty.
Some twenty summers since have flown,
  Leaving behind their ripening traces,
And Bessy to full stature grown,
  Now shines as lovely as the graces.

Her smile as bright as the morning ray
  That sparkles on the dewy blossom,
Would charm a thousand cares away,
  And into Lethe's bosom toss 'em;
A lily smiling at my feet,
  A priceless gem of purest water,
The morn ne'er dawned on flower so sweet,
  As bonny Bess, the Thatcher's daughter.

And 'tis beneath the straw-thatched cot,
  We see the sweetest damsels shining,
Contented with their humble lot,
  Seldom complaining or repining;
And like flowers that gem the moor,
  Or blossom in the shady valley,
That bright-eyed children of the poor,
  Oft charm us in the darkest alley.

Wells Journal, September 1865

---

[12] In September 1870 the following piece appeared in the *Wells Journal*: "Our obituary this week announces the death, at the early age of 26, of Elizabeth Savage, the daughter of a very honest and industrious couple residing in Tucker Street, Wells. It may, perhaps, be interesting to our readers to know that the deceased was one of the few rustic beauties immortalized by our own Baker Bard in his genial verses. The gentle demeanour and amiable disposition of the fair departed, seems to have operated like a ray of sunshine on the impressible heart of our poet and on one calm evening in 'Mellow Autumn-Tide' he seized his harp and presented her with the following graceful effusion which we copy from his *Morning Musings* just published".

NOVEMBER

The rain beats hard against the window pane
The yellow leaves are flying o'er the plain,
The wind roars wildly down the rain-washed lane,
And toilers crowd the ingle-nook again.
With winds and storms and thunder bolts beset
November strides along with streaming eyes,
Her hair dishevelled and her fingers wet
Crushing the flowers and clouding o'er the skies.
Old Neptune screeches like a tortured ghost,
The trembling landsmen hears the cracking mast
The hardy sailor shivers in the blast
And wrecks are multiplied along the coast.
Disease strikes down the ox to rise no more
And death is busy knocking on the door.

Wells Journal, October 1865

THE DRUNKARD

A hearty cheer for those who find
The path of life with roses lined!
Cares crowd the rugged way along,
And try thy weak and tease the strong;
But the greatest plague we know,
Is the teasing drunkard, O!

The poor man toiling for his bread,
With toil-drops oozing from his head,
Sun-burned and bronzed with wind and sun,
Can tell how hard his crust is won;
But the hardest thing we know
Is the hardened drunkard, O!

The bustling trader in his store,
Deems every doubtful debt a bore,
For while the debt uncancelled stands,
His money shines in other hands;
But the greatest bore we know,
Is the boring drunkard, O!

The farmer tills the stubborn land,
Manures and sows with liberal hand,
But seeks in vain for crops of grain
When blighting winds have swept the plain;
But the blackest blight we know,
Is the blighting drunkard, O!

The highway robber knocks you down,
And robs you of your hard-earned crown,
The burglar goes when all is still,
And leaves behind an empty till;
But the greatest thief we know,
Is the robbing drunkard, O!

No peace by day, nor rest by night,
No sunny faces round and bright,
No smile, no song within that cot,
Cursed by the lazy, slobbering sot;
For there's not a curse below,
Like the cursing drunkard, O!

Oh shameless sots! oh, drunken drones!
Your hearts are turned to flinty stones;
You've every holy feeling crushed,
And trampled conscience in the dust;
And there's nothing that we know,
Loathsome as the drunkard, O!

Shepton Mallet Journal, October 1865

POOR DOBBIN'S DEATH

"Just twenty minutes driving down,
So now we've got quite an hour to spare,
To ramble up and down the town,
Before they ope the House of Prayer."

The little whip who spoke so large,
Was such a gentle, Christian man,
That he of classes had the charge,
And figured on the preachers' plan.

A noted man he was indeed,
He prayed at morn, and preached at night,
And clung so closely to his creed,
That he was deemed a shining light.

Yet *self* absorbed his every care,
When he stood up, or when he knelt;
His kindness all oozed out in prayer.
And what he preached he never felt.

A living load of shining lights
Beside himself, he drove to town,
And sorely tried poor Dobbin's *lights,*
When rattling o'er the breezy down.

But he cared nought for legs, or lights,
But kept on slashing all the way,
And whisked along o'er Mendip's heights,
And whipped and kicked the panting bay.

So down they came, the pious lot,
  At racing speed into the city;
The used-up bay was steaming hot,
  An object of concern and pity.

Full seven long miles, and rather more,
  In twenty minutes, just for fun,
He made poor Dobbin's legs go o'er,
  And boasted of the feat he'd done!

The clock strikes nine, the house of prayer
  Is closed, and homeward is the word;
    The party to the Inn repair,
  And there alarming news they heard.

And hastening to poor Dobbin's stall,
  They see him rolling in the *fret:*
And now they pray, and cry, and squall,
  But Dobbin does no easier get.

Another plunge, and Dobbin dies!
  His agonies are o'er, he's still!
He'll never form his straw-bed rise,
  Nor climb again his native hill!

Oh! Christians, while you preach and pray,
  Have mercy on the beasts you rear;
    For every cruel act, they say,
    Is noted with an angel's tear!

Shepton Mallet Journal, November 1865

JOHN CROSS

The Dorsetshire labourer, a man with a large family, was sent to prison for stealing an old hurdle for firewood. His case provoked such a storm of indignation throughout England that nearly £300 was subscribed for him during his confinement.[13]

Away from Dorsetshire,
O'er meadow, mound and mere,
The wail of unrewarded labour comes;
Poor Cross's thrilling tale,
Born on the chilling gale,
Is telling in a thousand distant homes.

Within that crowded hive,
Nine precious souls contrive
To fast and feast on fourteen pence a day!
Yes burly, grasping Greed,
There's nine to clothe and feed,
And seven to rear with that poor toiler's pay!

Oh! think upon his lot,
And look into his cot,
And see his children shivering round the hearth,
Ye unsoiled, drowsy drones,
Strangers to weary bones,
And virtue learn from one of lowly birth.

Like Cross, rise with the sun,
And toil till day is done,
From year to year, for fourteen pence a day,
And grind an hard earned crust,
And rub away the rust
That daily gathers round your pampered clay.

---

[13] In November 1865 the *Wells Journal* reprinted a report from the *Daily Telegraph* describing Cross' imprisonment for stealing a wooden sheep hurdle worth 3d to use as firewood for his pregnant wife and seven children. Outrage at the harshness of Cross' punishment and sympathy for his plight was expressed in the pages of the *Wells Journal*: "Twenty five years of honest, faithful service to one master six days a week from daybreak to sunset. Grinding want, hopeless degrading misery, borne bravely till courage gave way at last. All these might have deemed palliations of John Cross's offences by the common man. But the Wimborne magistrates are not common men and they forthwith sentenced the hurdle stealer to 14 days hard labour. Well, as he has had five and twenty years already of hard labour, John Cross will probably look on his imprisonment as a holiday. His family will have eaten less while the breadwinner is in gaol; but by this time they must have got used to it as they are pretty well used to going without food at all. And what is more important still, hurdles, even when valued at 3d will henceforth be safe in the peaceful parish of Wimborne for the happy peasantry of Dorsetshire will be warned by the example of John Cross, the Oliver Twist of labourers, who, having a shilling a day and seven children to keep, actually wanted more".

Away! and guide the plough,
Or build the harvest mow,
Or drive the team along the Queen's highway,
Until the tear-drops shine
Upon your features fine,
And pay your way with fourteen pence a day.

Go out and till your lands,
Care not for blistered hands,
Nor feet well moistened with the morning dew;
Climb up the snow-crowned rick,
And serve your cattle sick,
And feel and feed like other workers do.

Your daily recompense,
Exactly fourteen pence,
And not a single mite or morsel more;
And then, and not till then,
You'll feel for other men,
And aid the labourer with your hoarded store.

Aye, try it just one week,
And don't get labour sick,
But think sometimes upon the men you hire;
'Tis right that you should know
The Worker's weal and woe,
And pass with him through Want's refining fire.

Wells Journal, December 1865

LIFE IN A LONDON BAKEHOUSE
(An Epistle to a Friend)

Bless me! You're going to London, eh?
Well 'tis a big and bustling place,
Where I've been toiling night and day,
With aching bones and haggard face.

I went at midnight's dreary hour
Down in the baking dungeon, close,
There, bathed in sweat I worked the flour,
And watched the sponges as they rose.

Two years and more of life's brief span
I toiled within and tramped without;
And true as I'm a living man,
I felt myself fast wearing out.

My tiresome round, twelve miles or more
As dusty as a miller's sack,
I walked until my feet were sore,
With galling basket on my back.

O'er the rattling, pitching stones,
In summer's sun and winter's sleet,
The barrow with my weary bones,
I pushed along the crowded street.

While friends and neighbours went to pray,
I cooked their Sunday meals below,
The baker knows no holiday
Between the bakings and the dough.

'Twas three o'clock each Sabbath day,
Before I'd washed, and dined and done,
Then on the bakehouse boards I lay,
While others dressed and had their run.

Thus rolled away the hours till six,
When I arose to set the sponge,
Almost too tired the flour to mix,
But little fresher for my lounge.

This done, t'was supper time, then o'er
The gas I boiled my "taters" nice,
Unrolled my bed upon the floor,
And slumbered with the rats and mice.

At twelve am, the masters bell!
Aroused me from my dusty nest;
I fancied sometimes t'was my knell,
But up I rose and did my best.

My faithful dog and loving cat
Both capered round me when I rose;
One jumped and rolled upon the mat,
The other danced upon my toes.

Fond comrades through the lonely night!
Tom on my pillow sat and purred,
And often made a breakfast light
On every rat or mouse that stirred.

And *Boxer* with his curly hide,
While on the bed or boards I lay,
Laid down at ease close by my side,
And warmed and watched me night and day.

With deep regret I left my pets,
But gladly bade the town adieu;
My earnings barely paid my debts,
And they indeed were small and few.

Thus manhood of its strength was shorn,
And blighted was its pride and bloom,
And bone, and brain, and muscle worn,
And weak, were trembling o'er the tomb.

Wells Journal, March 1866

THE MAN AND THE MOAT

I walked one eve beside the Palace Moat,
And as I strolled along, absorbed in thought,
Musing on sunny days long passed away,
I met a poor old man whose locks were gray;
He leaned upon his knotty, blackthorn staff,
And with a smile, which seemed but half a laugh,
He spoke of other days when he had strolled along,
Full forty years before, hearty and strong,
While tempting fruit hung on the cherry trees,
When fragrant flowers attracted honey bees,
When weeds were very few and very small,
And plums and peaches gemmed the Palace wall.
And then he sighed, and moved a step or two,
And said, "Whene'er the side walk now I view,
And see the box uneven and unshorn,
The gravel walk unweeded and unworn,
With weeds enough to hide the timid hare,
Or, cut and dried, to bed the farmer's mare,
And watch the fruit trees swaying to and fro,
Far as the rusted nails will let them go,
Exposed to every cutting breeze that blows,
I wonder if its noble owner knows,
How oft the gardener to the ruin goes,
To trim the walk, or train the blushing rose."
I wondered too, and wondering came away;
But everything, it seems, must have its day.

Wells Journal, May 1866

90

SONG TO THE MOWING MACHINE

Away! away! with speed away!
Among the meadow grasses
For mind! The longest summer day
If bright, too quickly passes,
And I've a pleasant task to do
Along the green sward dancing
Whilst in and out and out and in
My nimble teeth are dancing.

Away! away! with speed away!
My steeds are strong and steady
My driver cheerful as the day,
For mowing ever ready.
On, on from field to field I go
Defying hedge to follow,
Laying the grain and grasses low
On heath and holm and hollow.

Away! away! with speed away!
Trust not the fools "tomorrow"
For sunshine on a rainy day,
Is hard to buy or borrow
And though the summer sun is hot
And broad the farmer's acres
Ere sol goes down, the meadows lot
Shall wait the merry rakers.

Away! away! with speed away!
Heed not your thriftless neighbour
For brawny arms have had their day
And cunning conquers labour
The sinews of a dozen men
Are in my bosom lying
Ache, age, and toil defying.

Away! away! with speed away!
Among the tangled clover
The farmers work with me is play
And haying soon is over!
And I've a pleasant task to do
Along the green sward dancing
Whilst in and out and out and in
My nimble teeth are glancing.

Shepton Mallet Journal, June 1866

AWAY WITH MELANCHOLY

Away ye sentimental bores,
Ye sickly sonneteers,
Begone ye whining, doleful, pests,
Feasting on sighs and tears!
Distorters grim of Nature's face,
As miserable as vile,
Whose morbid minds are steeped in gloom,
Whose faces never smile.

Give me the verse where reason shines,
Where truth, though stern, appears,
Where fancy like a May day Queen,
The dress of Nature wears;
More genial than the breath of spring
More sweet than summer time
The line that gladdens as it flows,
The sunny bit of rhyme!

Let burning thoughts in cheerful words,
Like sunbeams, gild the page,
And every leaf emit a ray,
Of light for youth and age!
Let croakers grovel in the gloom
Their dismal lays have made
And common sense and reason join
To keep them in the shade.

The world is ripe with nobler thought
Than trembles on the tongue,
The world is full of melody
Unwritten and unsung,
The music of the march is sweet,
But action is sublime
And you may live a nobler verse,
Than can be told in rhyme.

Let lyres and lutes with tinkling breath,
To love-sick girls belong,
The rhythm of a well-spent life
Is sweeter far than song.
I'm weary of the waste of words
Our world were not so dead,
If half our bards would cease to write
And live their verse instead.

Wells Journal, July 1866

TO MARY ON RECEIVING HER PHOTOGRAPH

Mary! Thy precious gift today,
Demands from me a grateful lay;
But oh! Believe me every hour
I'm mixed up with so much dust and flour,
That I have had scarce a moments time
For jotting down a thought in rhyme.

Assist me, oh! My drowsy muse!
Thy choicest, sweetest, words to choose,
To ease a heart o'er brimming quite,
With such a flood of sweet delight,
That words like mine, can ne'er disclose,
The debt of gratitude it owes.

What shall I do, or write, or say,
Such loving kindness to repay?
May Heaven's blessing e'er attend thee,
May guardian Angels e'er defend thee,
May many prosperous years be thine,
And thy lot be happier far than mine.

Wells Journal, August 1866

EVENING

The mist is hovering o'er the stream,
Beneath the sun's last setting beam;
Along the banks the wild flowers bloom,
And shed their sweet perfume.

The weary swain, with toil oppressed,
Hies o'er the new-shorn fields to rest,
Whilst sighing through the leafy trees,
Is heard the dying evening breeze.

The landscape fades before the eyes,
The lover breathes his parting sigh,
The silent night its curtain draws,
And earth is hushed in calm repose.

Shepton Mallet Journal, September 1866

EVENING MUSINGS

The cold wind strips the yellow leaf,
The stars are twinkling faintly o'er us,
All nature wears the garb of grief
While day's fair book is clear before us.
Oh! in an hour or so still as this,
From care, and toils and tumult
I'll consecrate an hour to bliss-stealing
To sweet devotions holy feeling.

And rise to thee, to thee whose hand,
Unrolled the golden map of heaven
Mantled with beauty all the land,
Gave light to morn and hade to eve.
The being whose all-pervading might,
The laws of countless worlds disposes,
That gives the sparkling days their light,
Their beauty to the blushing roses.

Whose eye surveys creation vast,
And now the deeds of erring mortals,
Scanning the future and the past,
From earth's low vale to heaven's portals,
Though dark may be our path and damp,
Ten thousand stars shine sweetly o'er us,
And immortality's pale lamp,
Gladden and gilds the path before us.

Wells Journal, October 1866

THE WELCOME REDBREAST

I love the flowers, the marigolds,
The violets 'neath the apple tree;
The tints that Autumn's hand unfolds,
Heart-gladdening ever were to me.

I love to see the mellow fruit
Shine on the bending boughs again;
And now Spring's minstrels all are mute,
How dear to me the robin's strain!

I cannot tell how much I love
Its old familiar Autumn song;
Trilled in the garden or the grove,
It drops like honey from its tongue.

Concealed among the withered leaves,
The breeze is sweeping fast away,
The frost, the blast, it boldly braves,
And gaily pipes its loving lay.

Its little heart seems free from care,
Its bosom knows no grief nor guile;
Its songs gush forth as free as air,
As soft and sweet as beauty's smile.

From bower and brake, from bush and tree,
The zephyrs waft the notes along;
Notes fresh and pure, yet wild and free,
Compose its ever-welcome song.

And constant as the season comes,
It brings the robin and its lay;
I'll treat it with a feast of crumbs,
When Winter comes along this way.

Away! ye paid and petted drones,
Who sing God's praises for a fee;
The redbreast sings in sweeter tones,
Its anthem to the Deity.

Give me the music of the dells,
The chorus of the warblers wild;
More natural than the organ's swells,
And dearer far to Nature's child.

Shepton Mallet Journal, October 1866

THE WIDOW'S LITTLE BOY[14]

Where noble elms their shadows throw
Upon the gravel down below,
Beside the margin of the moat,
Where swans with graceful motion float,
And lovers tell their tales of love,
When moon-beams gild the towers above,
And bats around the ruins fly
Beneath the star-lit summer sky!

A Widow's boy, one sunny day,
Was dressed and kissed and sent to play
With several young companion's dear;
And there they viewed the water clear,
Ran, child like, round the towering trees,
Breathing the freshening, health-toned breeze,
That stole along beneath the boughs,
And fanned their little heated brows.

Brim-full of life they played that day,
No juvenile troop could be more gay,
They laughed and tumbled o'er and o'er,
And danced and capered more and more,
Without one care, or danger-thought,
Upon the borders of the moat,
Close to the very water's edge,
Unguarded by a rail or hedge.

---

[14] In September 1866 under the heading 'A Melancholy and Fatal Accident' the following news report appeared in the *Wells Journal*: "A sad accident which terminated fatally has happened to a little boy named Slade, the son of a widow living in Union Street. The deceased who was between the age of six and seven was with his sister who was carrying an infant around the Palace Moat and as the boy was walking along splashing the water to amuse the child, he missed his footing and fell in exclaiming, 'Oh! Emily.' The frightened sister ran for assistance but when persons came the body could not be seen. Ultimately a boat with the Bishop's servants arrived and recovered the body which was conveyed to the Police Station. Dr. Purnell was in attendance and endeavoured to restore animation but life was extinct. An inquest was held by the coroner and the jury returned a verdict of 'Accidental Death' and added to their verdict that it was a very dangerous place and recommended that something should be done to prevent the destruction of life, as the lives not only of children are endangered but persons on dark nights run a considerable risk. We have before commented strongly on the unsafe and unprotected state of the moat and we sincerely trust that those whose duty it is will see that a proper fencing is out round to prevent further loss of life". The wall around the moat was not built until 1877.

No more upon that pathway plain,
will that poor child e'er play again;
He toppled o'er the slippery bank,
And in the water deep he sank,
The rose, and shrieked, and sank again,
His playmates screamed, but all in vain:
Just where the diving ducks go down,
The Widow's boy was left to drown!

And now, when'er I pass that way,
When twilight shrouds the closing day,
I seem to see the drowning child,
That in the morn so sweetly smiled;
And hear the Widow's wail of woe,
And stop my ears, and on I go,
And hurry through the dangerous pass,
Dropping warm tears upon the grass.

There may, indeed, be none to blame,
No brows deep-crimsoned o'er with shame,
And none to justify the wrong;
But why not place some rails along,
And make it safe for boys and men,
Ere tolls some drowned one's knell again
Ere other hearts with grief are wrung,
And every drowned one finds a tongue?

Wells Journal, October 1866

AUTUMN

The robin comes to pick the crumbs,
And tell me in his winning way,
That summer's gone, and one by one,
The flowers are fading away.

No swallows dart o'er mead or mart,
'Neath brighter skies they twitter now,
No milkmaid's song the elms among,
Is heard upon the hillock's brow.

A drowsy lull, oppressive, dull,
Hangs like a curtain o'er the land,
And everything that used to sing,
Now cowers 'neath winter's threatening hand.

The little rills between the hills,
That lingered 'neath sweet summer's glow,
Now rush and roar towards the shore
Through brush and brake and moorland low.

Beneath the trees the biting breeze,
Is wailing through the weary night,
And branches bare and leaflets sere,
Are trembling in the morning light.

But winter o'er, spring buds once more,
Shall gem each meadow, bush and bough,
And song-birds sing, and flowerets spring,
And roses bloom round Labour's brow.

Wells Journal, November 1866

THE DISAPPOINTED WEDDING PARTY[15]

Young John and Joan, the papers say,
Quite tired of single life,
Had duly fixed the happy day,
To make them man and wife,
Provided brandy, beef, and beer,
And cake and custards new,
The hearts of coming guests to cheer,
And make them happy too.

The morn was fair, the sun shone bright,
The Bridegroom donned his best,
A brand new coat and breeches tight,
And many-coloured vest;
The Bride a beaded bonnet wore,
The newest pattern out,
A dress that cost ten bob or more,
And slippers strong and stout.

To church they went at half-past ten,
Exactly to the minute;
The clerk was there to say "Amen"
As lively as a linnet;
But the good Pastor, where was he?
Ah! where was he, I wonder?
Dancing the baby on his knee,
Down in the city yonder.

---

[15] In November 1866, the *Wells Journal* described the wedding-day of a young couple at the village church at Barton St. David in Somerset: "At eleven o'clock on that fateful morning these candidates for matrimonial honours repaired with an appropriate suite to their village church where the clerk met them and with accustomed politeness bade them good morning. After having wished them to be seated, he left them to themselves, to allow them no doubt time to prepare their minds for so momentous an occasion. We can hardly envy their feelings when after waiting until about 11.40am, no clergyman, or even the clerk had put in an appearance. The bridegroom at last determined to go and seek the missing but necessary functionaries. What must have been his state of mind on reaching the minister's residence and he heard the clock strike the dreaded hour of noon, which of course put an inseparable barrier in the way for that day at least? However, not to be entirely outdone, he returned to the church where the wedding party determined that the good things provided should not spoil for lack of consumption and they forthwith departed. The secret of this affair seems to have been a misunderstanding between the groom and the clerk. It is satisfactory to know that this slight interruption had no more serious effect on the parties most intimately concerned than to make them give the notice required and they tied the knot the following morning. It appears that the minster was about two miles from home on business, he not having the slightest idea that his services were needed."

They waited till their feet were cold,
They heard the church clock strike twice,
And fancied, somehow, they were sold,
Then homeward in a trice.
The baffled bridal party tore,
The maidens sighed and cried,
The burly Bridegroom stamped, and swore,
And wished the knot was tied.

At half-past twelve the parson came,
All in a streaming sweat,
And frankly owned he was to blame,
And deeply in their debt;
But ere the morrow's sun went down,
He'd bind them tight for life:
And so he did, he came from town,
And made them man and wife.

But why thus treat the labouring poor,
Who've little time to spare,
And make them wait outside the door
For hours, a-shivering there?
Don't ask me why. The priest, perhaps,
Who lives two miles away,
May say, he loves long morning naps,
And slept too long that day.

Wells Journal, November 1866

MARY ANN'S GRAVE

Oh! Lay her gently, gently down,
Amid the scenes she knew so well,
Within her dear old native town,
In her own lovely dell.

There let her slumber sweet and still,
With God's blue heaven o'er her spread,
Unvexed by aught of ache or ill
Among the quiet dead.

And o'er her, in the fair young spring,
How sweetly will the daisies wave,
And gladden summer sunbeams fling
Their splendours o'er her grave.

And gentle winds shall murmur low,
A sweet sad requiem as they pass,
And flowers their tear-filled urns will show
Among the wavering grass.

And spring-tide flowers she loved so well,
The violet and the primrose pale,
That charmed her in the dewy dell
And gemmed her own sweet dale.

We'll plant her place of rest,
To beautify the hallowed ground
To shine like stars upon her breast,
And shed their fragrance all around.

And when the Sabbath evenings gleam,
What Holy peace shall reign around!
How calm the settling sunlight stream
Upon that precious mound.

There may I lay me down at last,
Amid the scenes of life so dear,
The buds, the trees, the flowers, the grass,
And o'er me in Heaven's blue sphere!

Wells Journal, January 1867

PIOUS SUSAN

Oh, well! her happy spirits fled!
She's gone! But do not say she's dead:
Her exit from the scenes of earth,
Is but the spirits second birth
It's flight from earth to Paradise
Its early advent in the skies.
And while we view the lifeless clay,
The spirit lives in endless day,
Yet, tears of sorrow flow apace,
When musing on this child of grace,
And pensive fancy loves to view
The spot where pious Susan grew,
Where 'neath a loving parent's eye,
She breathed the prayer and heaved the sigh,
Watched o'er her heart with tender care,
And fondly nursed those graces rare,
Which brightened with each opening year.

Far from the thoughtless and the gay,
Who trifle life's brief span away,
She passed her rosy, youthful hours,
In verdant meads midst birds and flowers,
And rural objects fair and bright,
Where every blossom, bud and blade
That sparkled in the quiet glade,
And beautified the emerald sod,
Intensified her love to God.

Her prayerful breathings midst the flowers
In sultry summer's morning hours;
Her evening musings on the lawn,
Communing with her God alone;
Her soothing kindness to the poor,
Oft clustering round her father's door;
Her journey's to the house of prayer,
Her warm and deep devotion there,
Stand out before the mind's eye clear,
Making her name a memory dear,
Whose faith assures the aching breast,
That she has entered into rest.

So sweetly passed life's sunny morn,
That like a rose without a thorn,
Her virtues bloomed and shed abroad
Their rich perfume where're she trod.
But soon alas! consumption came,
And settled on her tender frame;
Then paled the brightness of that eye,
So oft upturned toward the sky;
Then from her cheeks the roses went,
But yet, her aspect spoke content,
And very word and motion showed
Her progress in the heavenly road,
And her devotion to her God.

Long months she lingered, yet her mind
Was to her Saviour's will resigned;
Her faith was strong, her hopes were bright,
And her pure soul glowed with the light
The Holy Book of Life supplies,
Which guides the pilgrim to the skies,
And daily as her slow decay,
Gave presage sure that life's faint ray
Would soon consume itself away,
Her happy spirit seemed to breathe
Heaven's purer air, and all beneath,
Appeared to her enlightened eye,
Scarce worth a tear or farewell sigh.

Yet warm affection's fire burned bright,
And 'twas indeed a moving sight,
To watch the heaving of that breast,
Which longed to see its kindred blest;
To view that dim, imploring eye'
Shed tears of deep anxiety;
And mark the fervour which she felt,
When for their sakes in prayer she knelt,
In accents sweet she spoke of heaven,
And told them all that life was given
To fit the spirit for its high
And glorious station in the sky.
She pitied those who madly trod
The downward path which leads from God,
And with a love that thrilled the soul,
She wept, and prayed, and felt for all.

E'en now in fancy's ear I hear
In winning language, soft and clear,
Her counsels to a brother dear,
A lovely boy of tender years,
Whose name was breathed in all her prayers,
And while around her neck he hung,
What burning words dropped from her tongue!
With tears of strong affection fell,
Ere she could bid the boy farewell!
Yet not for him alone she felt,
For many in her bosom dwelt,
Each sister fair and brother kind,
Was present to her prayerful mind,
But still the youngest seemed to share
Her fondest hope, and tenderest care,
And when her spirit soared away
Toward the realms of endless day,
It bore to Heaven her final prayer,
That he might one day meet her there.

Thus passed the mortal to the tomb,
The ransomed spirit to its home;
And now, while kindred hearts with grief are riven,
The young immortal dwells with God in Heaven.

Wells Journal, February 1867

THE SABBATH MORN

Now soothing is the welcome calm,
The stillness of the Sabbath morn,
'Tis something like celestial balm
Poured o'er the weary and forlorn.

It yields a sense of soft repose,
Which stealing gently o'er the breast,
Beguiles it sweetly of its woes,
And calms the passions down to rest.

Oh! 'tis indeed, a golden time
For weary souls to rest and pray,
To climb from earth to heavens' clime,
And banish every care away.

'Tis sweet to hear the bells invite
The pilgrim to the House of Prayer,
Sweet to invoke the Lord of Light
For strength the ills of life to bear.

And, oh! 'tis sweet to stand alone
And muse in Nature's Temple fair,
To deeply feel and humbly own,
That Nature's God is present there.

In musing mood, the prayerful mind
A joyous sense of freshness feels,
Mounts up through Nature unconfined,
And to the Court of Heaven steals.

The scenes of earth, though bright and fair,
Fail to arrest its upward flight,
It soars on pinions light as air,
And bends before the infinite.

Shepton Mallet Journal, February 1867

A WORD TO THE BAKER'S REPLY[16]

I hope the bakers scribbling foes
Have brought their labours to a close,
Said all they can to try and tease
And left them to their wonted ease
Let those who love to whine and write
Work in the bakehouse just one night.
Go, take their places at the trough,
And try their arms at making dough.
And when the wind comes from the south,
Stand before the oven's mouth,
Until their blood boils in their veins
And then complete the baker's gains;
Run with the barrow round the town,
When the drilling rain is pouring down
And bend their backs, for one short hour,
'Neath the heavy sacks of wheaten flour,
And then the baker's paradise
That looks so lovely in their eyes,
Would less and less enchanting seem,
And vanish like a morning dream.
Who ever knew a baker rich,
Or in Fame's Temple win a niche?
Bad debts, bad heath and broken rest,
Break down the strongest and the best;
Let those who write and jeer and scoff
At those who mould the "little loaf"
Lie down with weary bones each night
And rise before the morning light
To struggle with the vexing things
That from the baking business springs,
And then perhaps the tongue and pen
So hard upon those "dusty men"
Will tell a more congenial tale
And "weigh" them in a juster scale.

Wells Journal, March 1867

---

[16] In February and March 1867 the *Wells Journal* reported that several Wells bakers had been fined for selling short weight bread. Among them were Catcott and his brother, John; they were fined 7s 6d not for short weight, but for not having scales on which to weigh their bread at the point of sale. The *Journal* printed an eleven-stanza poem signed 'A poor man's wife' that attacked the "bakers in our market town" who "cheat the rich and poor alike": "If rich men hardly like to lose, | Five ounces of their bread, | How must the poor man miss the slice | From off his little spread". 'A Word to the Baker's Reply' appeared in the following issue.

A BAKER'S TOIL

Half the night, beside the day,
Bakers toil for little pay,
Trying muscle, bone and brain,
Straining every nerve and vein,
At the oven or the dough,
In the dungeons down below.

Mark their faces as they pass,
Blanched with sulphur, heat and gas;
Few, indeed are straight or stout,
Wearing, wearing, wearing out,
Till they prematurely die,
And in graves unhonoured lie.

See them creeping from their holes,
With your welcome breakfast rolls;
You on downy pillows slept,
They the silent watches kept,
Toiling through the dreary night,
To provide your breakfast light.

From the oven's mouth they go,
Through the rain and through the snow,
Dragging aching limbs along,
Unregarded by the throng,
Who repay their toil and care
With a cold and heartless stare.

Sabbaths come and pass away,
They must in the bakehouse stay,
They must break the Sabbath day,
They must neither rest nor pray,
Doomed to cook your mid-day meal,
Cursing hearts that cannot feel.

For the slaves across the main
You can breathe a doleful strain:
But the slaves you daily see
Toiling hard for you and me
Die unheeded on the road,
While you whine for those abroad.

Can't you aid these sons of care?
Can't you stop this wear and tear?
The employers soon will yield,
When the public take the field,
'Tis the pressure from without
That will bring a change about.

Can't you roast your bit of veal
For your Sabbath mid-day meal?
Can't you in your own bright pot,
Boil the bacon you have got,
Cook your beefsteak nice and brown,
In a corner of your own?

If the masters stint their pay,
Don't purloin their Sabbath day;
Let them have a taste of ease
Let them breathe the freshening breeze;
Give them all the blessed day,
Let them ramble, rest and play.

Wells Journal, March 1867

SEASONABLE STANZAS

O'er the sunny southern hills,
Young Spring is coming fast;
Melted snow, in rippling rills,
Is singing Winter's past!

Daisies deck the dales again
The throstle trills his lay;
Lambs skip o'er the greening plain
Stern Winter's passed away!

Buttercups along the lane,
Are smiling as we pass;
Violets peeping out again
Between the leaves and grass.

'Neath the bramble half concealed,
The primrose shows its face,
Gemming forest, fence and field,
And every sheltered place.

Far away from smoky towns,
I fain would wander free,
Ramble o'er the daisied downs,
And Nature's beauties see.

Listen to the blackbird's song,
Who seems to pipe for me;
Through the valley stroll along,
From care and envy free.

Watch the buds burst into bloom,
Beside the merry brook,
Leave awhile the papered room,
And study Nature's book.

Sweet the walk at eventide,
Along the meadow path,
With a sunny-tempered bride
Beside the scented heath.

And when the glorious Summer fills
The land with warmth and wealth,
Sweet to picnic on the hills,
And breathe the breeze of health.

Wells Journal, April 1867

THE ROSY LITTLE BAR-MAID

Seated chatting with a friend,
Sipping cider from the jug,
Telling stories without end,
In a corner neat and snug,
A lassie, sweet and sunny,
Like a fairy tripped along;
She looked as sweet as honey,
And she won from me a song.

Smiling as she came and went,
With her plump and rosy face,
Beaming brightly with content,
Brightening up the little place;
Softly she came with the tray
Where tabby *Tom* reposes,
And offered me a nosegay,
Composed of pale primroses.

Gratefully the flowers I took
And placed them in spring-water,
Noting down in memory's book
The postman's pretty daughter;
Ever, ever may she be
Bright and pure as she is now
Bearing life's crosses bravely
With a clear unclouded brow!

Wells Journal, April 1867

MAY

How fresh and gay comes charming May,
All fragrant with the rich perfume
Of Flora gay, in bright array,
Decked with a thousand flowers in bloom!
She speeds along with laugh and song,
And dances o'er the meadows green;
While songsters sweet the senses greet,
And hawthorns white adorn the scene.

I love to stray at close of day
Adown the dale where orchards bloom,
Away from the strife of city life,
And freely breathe their sweet perfume.
'Tis sweet to roam away from home,
From business and its many cares,
To spend a day 'midst flowerets gay,
And view the dree which Nature wears.

The leafy trees fanned by the breeze,
Disclose their beauties to the eye,
And everything now seems to sing
Its anthem to the smiling sky.
Oh! lovely May! prolong thy stay,
Thy balmy fragrance and thy flowers;
The gladdened heart regrets to part
With thee, for summer's sultry hours.

Wells Journal, April 1867

EVENING

I love the quiet evening hour,
The soft repose of day's decline,
'Tis then the Muse exerts her power,
And every object seems divine.

There is a calmness in the air,
A sense of sweetness as we move,
Which fills the soul with visions rare
Of that mysterious world above.

And while the stars are peering forth,
And every flower its dewdrop bears,
The spirit soars above the earth,
And for a time forgets its cares.

I love the hallowed evening hour,
Its soothing stillness calms the breast;
It is the weary spirit's dower,
Its season sweet of Sabbath rest.

Wells Journal, May 1867

PRETTY POLLY FEAR

Oh! a daisy blossom sweet,
Is pretty Polly Fear,
With her little pattering feet,
And her flaxen-coloured hair!
She's her mother's pearl of pearls,
And her daddy's darling doll,
And the queen of rosy girls
Is loving little Poll.

She's brimful of winning ways,
And happy as the day,
Singing easy, simple lays
In her own amusing way;
And there's something in each tone
Of the winsome warblers notes
Makes the saddest spirit own,
She has brightened up its thoughts.

And we long to see her face
Lit up with smiles again,
For she keeps alive the place
With her spirit-touching strain.
Oh, a daisy-blossom bright
Is pretty Polly Fear,
Opening in the morning light,
Pure, fragrant, fresh and fair!

Wells Journal, May 1867

THE SHEPTON MALLET ODD FELLOWS' FESTIVAL

Behold, the grand procession's formed!
I'm sure you'll with the sight be charmed
The banners now are waving high,
And scenes of beauty meet the eye;
The brethren dressed and trimmed so smart
You see are about to start;
The streets are crowded and the band
Is waiting for the Noble Grand.
Well, now they're off, and I declare
They've made the very children stare;
We used to think the clubs "a sight"
But this has beaten them outright
All two and two in one long row,
Along the streets to church they go,
And how their glittering medals shine,
Their aprons too, how wondrous fine
What pretty, costly things they are!
Such sashes, well, why I declare
They've purple, scarlet, plaid and pink
But blue predominates I think.
Beside they've gloves and gauntlets too
Rosettes of almost every hue,
And collars from the mercers new;
And as they pass between the lines
How bright their fine regalia shines!
The sacred volume borne along
Adds grace and beauty to the throng,
And let us hope they've conn'd it o'er
And pondered well its precious lore

Its hallowed precepts learned by rote
And blended them with every thought.
And see, what in a curious way
Their hands white-gloved are joined today,
The little finger of each man
Is bent in such an odd like plan
That in two loving links they join.
Each file along the lengthy line,
And as they pass with happy hearts
The scene, a gleam of joy imparts
To wondering thousands as they gaze
And greet them with their honest praise.
'Tis beautifully "odd" to me
To see this old fraternity.
Such powerful love to each display
As I have witnessed here today
And this I'll own, I've seen a sight
That's filled me with intense delight.
And while the eye delighted views
The splendour of their rainbow hues
The "small still voice" proclaims the worth
Of these enlightened sons of earth;
Points to the widow's brightening eye
Tearless and sunny as the sky,
And shows the chamber of disease
With the pale sufferers' mind at ease
Each soothed by their fraternal aid,
And happy in the sun or shade.

Shepton Mallet Journal, June 1867

MY VILLAGE HOME

I see before my mind's eye, bright and clear,
My village home beside the hazel wood,
Where oft in youth's hey-day, I've musing stood,
Enchanted with the scenes presented there.
I've looked down the slope and watched the brook,
Between the hills, glide down through the willowed vale,
Observed the lambs disporting in the dale,
And learnt sweet lessons there from Nature's book.
I see the breezy windway and the rock,
Where oft returning from the crystal well,
Has sat the weary, rosy village belle;
I see the pond, the shepherd, and the flock,
But oh! I hear the city's din and strife,
Which call me from the scenes of early life.

Wells Journal, July 1867

THE HARVEST AGAIN

Oh! the light summer breeze,
As it steals through the trees,
Freshening the mountain, the meadow, and plain,
Wandering slowly along,
Breathes again the old song,
The harvest is come, the harvest again!

In spring's dawn, the green blade
Crowns the plough and the spade,
That comes the ear bending down with its grain,
Then the reapers begin,
And our warm wishes win,
Merrily shouting, the harvest again!

Now the sheaf and the hile,
Makes the stout farmer smile,
And soon the strong team will come with the wain,
And the sheaves bear away
In the bright sunny day,
And safely garner the harvest gain.

Now fair gleaners in troops,
Come without any hoops,
And follow the wake of the corn-laden wain,
O'er the stubble fields haste,
Gathering up all the waste,
Cheerily singing, the harvest again.

Let the rich and the poor
Join their voices once more,
And unite in a sweet thanksgiving strain,
To the Giver above,
Who has sent us in love
The fruits of the earth, the harvest again.

Wells Journal, August 1867

THE ROBIN

Among the apple trees
Whose blossom feeds the bees,
Where fine fruit lately hung
And summer warbler sung,
The robin comes today
To trill his autumn lay.

And oh! the song he trills,
My little garden fills
With music soft and sweet
While I sit at his feet
And muse away the hours
Among the fading flowers.

And while I sit and sigh,
To see the leaflets die
And watch the flowers decay
There's something in thy lay
Sweet bird, that seems to tell
All things are ordered well.

Upon the housetop high,
Or on the yew tree nigh,
Or 'tween the kidney beans
Or 'mongst the winter greens,
Beside thy path along
Oh! come and sing thy song.

When icy winter comes,
I'll feed thee well with crumbs,
And well wilt thou repay
Me with thy cheering lay,
And happy I shall be
With such a guest as thee.

Wells Journal, September 1867

AUTUMN BREEZE

The breeze blows fresh o'er Mendip's famous hills,
Dark lowering clouds now sweep across the sky,
And Autumn's glories wane beneath the eye,
But yet, the fading prospect charms, and thrills
And fills the mind with pleasing hopes, and visions bright,
Of coming evenings, pregnant with delight.
Each season has its charm; the flowery spring
Perfumes the air; productive summer rears
The golden sheaf, which autumn on the wing
Matures, repaying all the toiler's cares,
And filling hearts with gratitude intense.
I love thee, Autumn! beauteous in decay!
Thou art the labourer's hope and recompense,
Which cheer when summer's flowers have passed away.

Wells Journal, September 1867

THE CAT AND HER TORMENTOR

Ye noble hearts with kindness swelling
Listen to the tale I am simply telling:
It is no fiction but a fact
Which makes my heart strings nearly cracked.

The untamed brute that roams the earth,
Or tamely sits beside the hearth,
No matter what its kind or worth,
Most justly claims its destined share
Of all the kindness we can spare;
And he must be unrighteous quite,
Who would the laws of nature slight
And fiend-like torture with delight,
The meanest creature in his sight.

Not long ago a gardener took
A friendless cat, they called her "old Suke"
And placed her safe 'neath lock and key;
Till he had starved her life away.
Her cries each morn and eve he heard,
But nothing in his bosom stirred,
Fourteen long days, or rather more,
The poor thing mewed inside the door,
While he was mocking at her cries,
And grinning at her glossy eyes,

By inches did she starve and die
Beneath that cruel gardener's eye;
He heeded not her wailing plaint
Which came each day more low and faint;
But when her bones came through her skin
Her stern tormentor then went in
And saw her, still and stiff and dead;
"Thou art gone at last" he gruffly said,
The threw her in the Palace Moat
And whistling went for want of thought.
But he who marks the sparrow's flight
Whose ear is open day and night,
Who hears the unfledged ravens cries,
And from his stores his wants supplies,
Has numbered all her hunger-cries
And registered her agonies,
And written down in lines of flames
Against the gardeners' name
His sentence of disgrace and shame.

But I must pause, nor dare presume
To meddle with the wretches doom;
In simple words, I've told my painful story,
If you don't feel for puss, I'm sorry for ye.

Wells Journal, October 1867

THE COMING OF AGE OF CHARLES CLEMENT TUDWAY[17]

What means those bonfires bright,
Upon the hills tonight?
What makes the bells in old St Cuthbert's Tower,
Such merry music make,
And dreaming sleepers wake,
Ere yet the clock has chimed morn's youngest hour?

What makes the cannons roar,
Unused for years before,
To usher in this dull November day?
What makes the mansion seem
Like some young fairies dream
O'er brimming with the gayest of the gay?

See ye that fair young squire,
The ladies so admire,
Presiding at the board with dainties piled:
For him the bells were rung,
For him sweet songs were sung,
For he is Tudway's heir and only child.

Today on manhood's stage,
He claims his heritage,
A rich domain of meadows, down and dells
And fine old game preserves,
Where sportsmen try their nerves
And sunny fields a thousand miles from Wells.

Today to manhood grown,
He fills his father's throne,
And sways the sceptre o'er his vast estate,
May happiness' and health
Be added to his wealth
And Wells be blessed with both good and great.

And may he ne'er forget
The debt, uncounted yet,
His mother claims for all her watchful care;
And may she live to see
Her honoured darling be
A brilliant star in his exalted sphere!

Wells Journal, November 1867

---

[17] The Tudway family lived at the Cedars in the Liberty in Wells; they were local landowners and plantation owners in the West Indies.

TO A PRIMROSE IN NOVEMBER

Fair ever-welcome thing,
Reminding me of spring,
And telling how the seasons roll along!
I loved thee when a boy,
Far better than a toy,
And oft hast thou inspired me with a song.

Shining among the leaves,
Beneath the cottage eaves,
Thy glory gleams beneath the elder bough;
Where summer blossoms shone,
Thou shinest all alone
To crown with beauty Autumn's fading brow.

Sweet memories dost thou bring
Of pleasant walks in Spring,
Beside the one I loved, so fond and fair;
And still her spirit seems,
To meet me in my dreams,
Bright as the seraph's in a brighter sphere.

The land beyond the tomb,
Where flowers immortal bloom,
Where rills of perfect bliss for ever flow,
And sundered spirits meet
In holy union sweet,
And parting, pain or sorrow never know.

May no destroying shower,
Its fury on thee pour,
Nor biting frosts thy opening blossoms close!
Still grow, and bud, and blow,
Through Winter's sleet and snow,
Till Spring her vest o'er field and forest throws.

Passed winter's stormy reign,
We then shall see again,
The meadow banks starred o'er with millions more;
And then will music gush
From every bower and bush,
And gladdened hearts creation's God adore.

Wells Journal, November 1867

REMINISCENCE

Oh where are the fond ones I loved to have near me,
Whilst nought but the pleasures of childhood I knew,
Oh where are the scenes that at all times could cheer me
Ere yet to the vigour of manhood I grew.

These eyes are the same as that youth's early morning,
Beholding so much that around them seemed bright,
Saw nought but enjoyment nor heeded the warning,
The beautiful gives when it fades from the sight.

From the fond ones I'm severed by death or by distance,
The scenes of my youth but in memory live,
For the strongest time can offer no resistance,
And the joys of this would have no pleasures to give.

But oh, there are pleasures and joys without number,
Far better that those that have gratified here
In the Kingdom to come, where no sorrow will cumber,
And God from each face shall wipe off every tear.

Wells Journal, December 1867

"ONE STORY'S GOOD TILL T'OTHERS TOLD"

How oft will gossips meet and prate,
To injure those of low estate,
And every floating rumour tell,
And every whispered folly swell
Forgetting, while they scoff and scold,
One story's good till t'others told.

But did they feel the harm they do,
Their meetings surely would be few
Their wasted hours be better spent
Is closing up some garment rent,
Or pondering on the truth I hold
One story's good till t'others told.

But when we see the professing men
Resorting to the tattler's den,
And muttering there their slanders vile,
The Arch Deceiver sure must smile
To see them shirk the truth I hold
One story's good till t'others told.

Their victim there they blacken o'er,
And his defence they deem a bore;
One side, and only one, they hear,
And then their sentence pass severe,
Disdaining thus the truth I hold,
One story's good till t'others told.

To carry out their blasting plan,
They gather all the lies they can,
And sow them broad-cast as they go,
In every alley, street and row,
Scorning the maxim which I hold,
One story's good till t'others told.

Just say the dog that passed you by,
Is mad, and he is doomed to die;
Backbiters play their games the same,
And wound and slay devoid of shame,
Hating the truth I always hold
One story's good till t'others told.

Oh! what a blessed thing t'would be,
If mischief-makers could but see,
Displayed without the least disguise,
The sad effects of all their lies,
And learn the blessed truth I hold
One story's good 'till t'others told.

The Judges of the land, we know,
My maxim prize where're they go;
And to each party show fair play,
Confirming thus the truth I hold,
One story's good till t'others told.

Cornubian and Redruth Times, December 1867

DEAR LITTLE ALFRED,
YOUNGEST SON OF JOHN HARRIS, THE CORNISH POET

Away down in the sunny west,
A bright-eyed boy was born to-day;
I seem to see him in his nest,
Although so many miles away.
He's eight years old this very day,
And brimming o'er with life and glee,
Yet loves his books, as well as play;
His father's darling boy is he.

A noble heritage is thine
Dear boy, won by thy gifted sire,
Who sweetly sang his songs divine,
And thrilled the nation with his lyre.
Though lowly-born, his honoured name,
Made ever-glorious by his pen,
Shines brightly on the scroll of fame,
Above the reach of high-born man.

Thine is a blessed lot, my boy,
And well may thousands envy thee;
Thy father's pride, thy mother's joy,
The youngest of the family.
No thorny cares yet cross thy way,
No shadow rests upon thy brow;
But, like a flower in merry May,
Thou smilest in the sunshine now.

O may thy onward course be bright,
Thy years be full of happy days;
Thy cares and crosses few and light,
And thy whole life be one of praise,
To Him who dwells above the skies,
Who loves the seeker after truth,
Who ever guides the good and wise,
And smiles upon the pious youth.

Wells Journal, February 1868

128

FANNY'S GIFT

How sweet the cowslips smell,
Down in the quiet dell,
Where violets coy, and white-rimmed daisies grow;
Where buttercups display
Their beauties day by day,
And primroses their spring-tide glories show!

Amongst the floral gems
That shine like diadems
Upon the meadow banks in March and May;
The cowslip on the lea
The fairest seems to me,
Smiling and nodding o'er the field pathway.

Within the cottage room,
How sweet is its perfume!
We hail the golden glory of the spring,
Where'er we chance to meet,
In meadow, lane, or street,
Beside the hearth, or where the wild birds sing.

Upon my table stands
One fresh from fanny's hands,
Gathered and given in her genial way;
The fragrant flower I prize,
And bless its yellow eyes,
And hail it as the brightest bud of May.

Upon the flower I gaze
In twilight's dreamy haze,
Until the smile which brightened Fanny's brow,
When parting with the flower,
In all its winning power,
I see again, and oh! I see it now.

I see a rosy face
That would a palace grace,
A form on which the eye delights to dwell;
And think, and think again,
How blest will be the swain,
That woos and wins the lively little belle.

Wells Journal, April 1868

DRUNKEN NED'S SOLILOQUY

They say that I'm a drunken beast,
  'Tis true for ale I've got a taste;
  But still I'm not so bad as some,
  Say what you will, 'tis all a hum.

  'Tis very hard, indeed, I think,
  That I can't taste a drop of drink,
And spend the night just where I choose,
  But master stuns me with abuse.

But let him scold, I'll heed him not,
  My mind's made up to be a sot;
  I do not care if both lips crack,
  Nor if my crimson nose turns black.

Why should I care? my money's mine,
  To let me in the tap-room shine,
And smoke my pipe and treat my pals,
  And spend my money on the gals.

Oh! those sweet gals, so kind and smart!
  How oft they captivate my heart!
Whene'er they whisper, Ned, my dear,
  I call for lots of gin and beer.

Though some may laugh at foolish Ned,
  I'll not retract a word I've said;
  I'll drain the pewter while I can,
  And be a glorious drunken man.

I do not care what clothes I wear,
  If feet and back and head are bare;
Give me some beer to warm my nose,
And those who will may care for clothes.

At each week's close my money goes,
  And then commences all my woes;
I'm forced to scheme, and sometimes steal,
  To get another pint of ale.

Besides, I've got a mother old
And sick, as I've been often told;
And if I could a trifle save,
'Twould smooth her passage to the grave.

But she may starve for what I care,
While I am gulping down strong beer;
I scorn to lay a penny by,
I won't, I can't, I'm always dry.

I used to think I'd got a soul,
But I'm got blinder than the mole,
And now the only thing I know,
Is that my pocket's always low.

They say that when a drunkard crokes,
Old Nick in fire his spirit pokes;
That seems to me a darkish tale,
But I'd go anywhere for ale.

I used to keep the Sabbath day
In something like a proper way;
But now I ne'er to worship goes,
I can't, I've swallowed all my clothes.

So now, as fast as Sunday comes,
In spite of mother's prayers and hums,
I stagger to some alehouse near,
And soak my carcase well with beer.

And should I in some workhouse die,
With no bright lass or landlord nigh,
Oh, place a beer-glass o'er my head,
To mark the dust of Drunken Ned!

Wells Journal, May 1868

OH TELL ME NOT OF DREARY THINGS

Oh tell me not of dreary things
Of scenes of saddening woe,
Nor breathe a whisper of a tale
A gloomy shade may throw.
My heart is light, my soul is glad
That man despite the ills of life
Was made for joyous ends.

What through disease may lay me low,
Dark clouds obscure the day,
Old friends prove false, or droop and ide
And foes beset my way;
My spirit still rise and bear me up
Above the gathering gloom,
My thoughts soar up to realms above,
Where flowers forever bloom.

Go to! ye drivellers of the world
Ye cankers of the mind
Who say that sorrow, only sorrow,
Is the human kind.
Away! there's blackness on your brows,
And sadness in your eyes;
Your bony cheeks are blanched with care,
Your bosoms crammed with sighs.

Away! the mind itself can mould
The brightness of its fate,
Can summon up the beautiful,
To cheer it soon or late,
Can calmly view portentous clouds,
That hover o'er life's blue sky,
And smile, serene, amid the strife
Of woe that rushes by.

The summer's soothing zephyr breath,
The insect in its flight,
The orb that rules the mid-day sky,
The splendours of the night,
The very kitten of your heart
Thy gloominess would scorn;
Would playfulness and beauty teach,
Man was not made to mourn.

Away! ye nervous-hearted ones,
Shrink from the free souls scorn,
'Tis false; we fling it in your teeth
That "man was made to mourn."
For on the earth in youth and age,
With power that may not cloy,
Up to the tomb's dark verge we know
That "man was made for joy."

Wells Journal, October 1868

SONNET TO WILIAM BUDD, ESQ, M.D., CLIFTON[18]

It seems, sometimes, a blessing to be ill,
To test the Doctor's kindness and his skill
To try the strength and warmth of friendship's ties,
And draw the tear from sympathetic eyes.
Kind-hearted friends from hamlet, town, and dell,
Flock to my old thatched cot, and wish me well;
And thou, great master of the healing art,
Has nobly played the good Physician's part,
Relieved my aching breast of anxious thought,
And cheered and charmed me with a precious note.
O, for this priceless gem, what can I say?
My simple words its worth can never pay;
And to life's end thy debtor I shall be,
And bless the generous hand outstretched to me.

Wells Journal, October 1868

---

[18] Dr. William Budd was Catcott's physician during his stay at the West of England Sanatorium. In his early career Budd practised at the Bristol Royal Infirmary and he is credited with improving Bristol's water supply and decreasing the incidence of cholera in the city; he understood that the poisons present in infectious diseases were excreted and transmitted through the drinking of contaminated water.

"POOR OLD PARFITT"

But yesterday he faced the oven's mouth,
As he had done for more than fifty years;
And now, in yon green field toward the west,
They've laid him down to rest. From Life to death
How short the road! To-day in blooming health
To-morrow, in the unknown spirit land.
He toiled, without a murmur, lengthy days,
Through Summer's heat and Winter's sleet and snow,
And never turned his back towards his task,
But bravely worked on to the very last.
An even-tempered, kind, contented man.
When free from aching bones he went to church,
But oftener stretched his limbs upon the bed,
And prayed, and blessed the Lord for Sabbath rest.

Wells Journal, October 1868

I'M SOMETIMES SAD

I'm sometimes sad, and yet I am calm;
There is in quietness a balm
Which soothes my watery spirit lone,
I cannot mingle with the gay,
Nor flutter through the world like they,
But yet I've pleasures all my own.

I cannot bend my spirit down
To cringe behind the bigot's frown,
Nor greet the tyrant with a smile;
Nor can I sympathise with those
Who would the poor man's rights oppose,
And force him to the cloistered aisle.

I've seen, with pain, the sons of need
Unjustly punished for their creed,
And seen the tear of anguish wrung,
From simple hearts, with kindness fraught,
For jotting down an honest thought,
Or speaking freedom with the tongue.

I cannot smile at deeds like these,
Nor bribe my soul the vile to please,
Nor will I wield a flatterer's pen;
I scarce had passed the days of youth
Ere I was scorned for telling truth,
I was indeed, and may again.

I do not like the din and strife,
The wear and tear of city life,
For there the mind has little rest;
The city has no charms for me,
I love the fields, for there I'm free,
And rural pleasures please me best.

I love to ramble on the hills,
From whence gush forth those murmuring rills,
Which fertilize the valleys fair;
I love to hear the sheep-bells' tone
Upon the mountains wild and lone,
And breathe the freshening zephyrs there.

I love the hills, the dales, the streams'
The radiant sun's bright morning beams,
And mellow evening, soft and grey;
To me the twilight hour is dear,
And starry evenings calm and clear,
And Luna's pale and silvery ray.

There's something in the landscape fair,
In Winter's gloom and Summer's glare,
That yields a sense of gladness rare;
For in the prospect, bright, serene
The loving hand of God is seen,
Inspiring hope and soothing care.

Wells Journal, November 1868

SIXTEEN SUMMERS

Long have I gazed upon her charms
And mused upon her virtues bright,
In fancy held her in my arms,
And felt sweet thrills of pure delight;
Lay after lay I have composed,
And breathed soft music in her ear,
Laid wide awake while others dozed
And offered up warm prayers for her;
In every hour, in every place
My heart has throbbed for her alone,
Enchanted with a form and face
I'd give up all my worlds to own.

Gay dames may flutter and may fade,
While dandies strut and gas lamps shine,
Reserve for me, the rustic maid
Sweet as her own sweet eglantine;
Endowed with wit and common sense,
And thrifty as the busy bee,
Early each day her toils commence,
And care and want before her flee.
No gloomy thoughts disturb her rest
Or find an entrance to her breast.

Wells Journal, March 1869

MARCH

Here comes young blustering March,
Duly prepared to search,
And try the feeble cot-bound invalid,
Shaking with giant hand
The trees that deck our land,
Scattering the hail in yonder storm-cloud hid.

Sometimes he makes his bow
With daisies on his brow,
And buds and blossoms on the bushes show,
Luring the birds to lay,
In nests of moss and hay,
The, laughing, fills them up with snow.

Braving the blast, we see
The primrose on the lea,
And down the lane the fragrant violet rears
Its little purple head
Above its leafy bed,
And every hedge its greening mantle wears.

And soon the lowing cows,
Now clustering round the mows,
And teasing Hodge, at morn and even-tide,
Will feed in pastures green,
Where cowslips sweet are seen,
And lambkins gambolling o'er the meadows wide.

Between the drops of rain
The farmer sows his grain;
The thrifty toiler to the garden hies
When day is near its close,
For every seed he knows,
Will tell its tale 'neath April's warmer skies.

Then, blow away, rude March!
Each nook and corner search,
And chase and sweep the seeds of death away;
Let thy pure freshening breath
Be felt on hill and heath,
And rosy cheeks shall crown the windy day.

And flowers shall gem the dale,
And lovers tell their tale,
And every bower and bush with love-notes ring;
And grateful hearts combine
To sing a song divine,
To usher in the harbinger of Spring.

Wells Journal, March 1869

HAVE MERCY ON THE CALVES[19]

Have mercy on the calves,
Ye low-browed torturing knaves;
Nor bruise, nor bleed the harmless things
And if their lives are short
Show them you've a feeling heart,
And honour Him who made calves and kings.

I've seen the close-drawn string
Their swelling noses wring,
When driven, staggering to the market town,
And known their mouths tied tight,
From noon till morning light
And seen them lying panting on the down.

And watched the suffering cow,
Laden with milk enow,
To fill her offspring's belly twice or more
Stand moaning with the pain
Of the unnatural strain,
Until the moan has ended with a roar.

From every teat has flowed,
The milk upon the road;
Her udder swollen to twice its natural size,
The farmer viewed with pride,
And called his dame aside
And said; "Old Bride will fetch a stunning price."

---

[19] In the *Wells Journal* of March 1865 a letter appeared which highlighted the distress caused to calves by the practise of bleeding them to make their meat white: "I wish to call the attention of your readers to the practise of bleeding calves to make their flesh white. The butchers say that they cannot sell the veal unless it is white and yet I will not believe the humane public of this Christian land willingly and wilfully uphold this wicked system. Surely those who insist upon having their veal white do so in ignorance. They must be ignorant of the fact that this white meat is purchased over the price of protracted torture extending over some days. To quote the words of a local butcher; 'They oblige us to bleed the calves till it makes even a butchers heart ache. On going into a calf house and seeing the poor creatures lying fainting, more than half dead for days before slaughter it makes the human heart bleed.' English ladies and gentlemen shall this continue? Will you any longer be responsible for this monstrous wrong? Surely this barbarous treatment of an inoffensive creature to satisfy a whim of luxury is an offence against our Maker and a foul crime against humanity".

The "bobby" dealer now,
Takes his "bobby" from the cow
And kicks and hunts it miles and miles to town,
Or swearing, strikes it hard
And ties its legs with cord,
And sometimes bleeds it well to keep it down.

With legs and mouth tied tight,
They race along by night,
And shake and bruise them on the hard, rough road,
But why inflict such pain
And mercy's banner strain
When you might move with ease your living load?

Have those no hearts to feel,
Who deal in calves and veal?
Why tie and toss and jerk the young things so?
Surely you ought to know
That they can feel each blow
Then pause, and let your breast with mercy glow.

Ye officers in blue!
Be to your colours true
And make torturers dread the judgement seat.
Search every blood-stained cart
The heartless dealers start
And drive the torture mongers from your beat.

Wells Journal, March 1869

THE HOME NURSE[20]

A charming nurse, indeed is Emily
So loving and so kind,
The gem of our sick family
The best and gentlest of her kind!

Designed by Nature for the place,
She toils in this sweet Home of ours,
We hail her with joy, her rosy face
And fain would strew her path with flowers.

With smiles she greets us day by day
And nurses us with skill and care,
With smiles she steals our hearts away
And charms us with her virtues rare.

Oh Emily! We ne'er can tell
How much to thee we daily owe,
But this we know, when we get well
Our hearts with thankfulness will glow.

And like an angel from the skies,
When we are gone and far away
Thy form will flit before our eyes,
And cheer us like a sunny ray.

And oft, when musing on the "Home"
What wishes pure and warm will rise,
For blessings on thy years to come,
For health and bliss beyond the skies.

Wells Journal, May 1869

---

[20] In 1869 Catcott's health began to fail and he went to the West of England Sanatorium in Weston-super-Mare to convalesce. "The West of England Sanatorium is situated on the Uphill Road about one mile from Weston super Mare with the green fields and the Mendip Hills in front and the Atlantic Ocean in the rear. It is approached by a veranda on which is arranged a selection of choice shrubs and flowering plants. On entering the visitor finds himself in a spacious dining hall, appropriately furnished, on either side of which are the apartments of the officials connected with the home. ...Among the patients we recognised one familiar face, the cheerful Baker Bard of Wells who is suffering from dropsy. His smiling visage pays testament to the comfort of the Home" (*Wells Journal*, June 1869). See also 'The Home Nurse,' 'Bonny Bess, the Happy Housemaid,' 'An Ode, Written at the West of England Sanatorium, Weston-super-Mare,' 'Carrie, the Merry Orphan Maid,' and 'Our Convalescent Cook.'

BONNY BESS, THE HAPPY HOUSEMAID

Oh! Bessy; let me sing a song,
A cheerful song for thee,
And let us stroll the flowers among,
Beside the honey bee;
Together breathe the morning breeze,
While sings the lark on high,
While May-buds gem the daisied leas
And swallows round us fly.

And let us on the green bank stand,
And see the flowing tide
Come rushing o'er its bed of sand,
In all its power and pride;
And watch the setting sun go down
Beyond the great wide sea,
Flooding with glory, tide and town
And terrace, tower and tree.

And let me hear thy hearty laugh
Come ringing o'er the lawn
And tread with thee the meadow path
With many daisies strewn;
And look into thy loving eyes
So black, so beautiful and bright,
And pray to Him beyond the skies
To bless thee with love and light.

Wells Journal, 11 June 1869

AN ODE,
WRITTEN AT THE WEST OF ENGLAND SANATORIUM, WESTON-SUPER-MARE

Beside the ocean's foam
The convalescent home,
Unfurls its banner on the sunny sand,
The suffering invalid
Finds it a home indeed
Where kindness, skill and care go hand in hand.

Aye 'tis a place of rest,
Facing the balmy west
When breezes from the hills beyond the sea
With cheering voices come,
Like angels to our Home
Bronzing the cheek and making sickness flee.

A blessed sweet retreat,
From labours dust and heat
Where care ne'er dares his haggard face to show
Where faces thin and white
Grow rosy, round and bright
And gladdened hearts with gratitude o'erflow.

How sweet at dewy dawn,
To stroll around the lawn
And breathe the odour of the smiling flowers,
Or on the terrace stand
And view the sea and land
And growing Weston's villas, trees and towers.

And when the flowing tide
Comes rolling, roaring on
How freshening to the limbs
The bracing brine bath seems
Warming to the heart and making eyes shine bright.

From far and near they come,
For health to our "sweet Home"
May blessing rich and rare from heaven flow down
On those who toiled to rear
For us a Home so dear
And with success their aims and wishes crown.

Wells Journal, June 1869

CARRIE, THE MERRY ORPHAN MAID

I met her at the water-side,
Upon the sunny strand;
The flowers of May were in their pride,
And Summer near at hand.

Her eyes were black as any sloe,
Her cheeks were fresh and fair;
She seemed a seraph sent below,
To bless the Son's of care.

Kind words, pure as the breath of morn,
Were gushing from her heart,
Cheering the languid, sick and lorn,
And soothing sorrow's smart.

Within the "Home" among the sick,
I watched her winning ways,
And heard her step, so soft and quick,
For many nights and days.

And ah! I still remember well,
How she could laugh and sing,
And swing about the dinner bell,
And make the welkin ring.

She placed the joint upon the board,
She filled our cups with ale,
And thanked and blessed her loving Lord
For every dainty meal.

She shook and smoothed our beds with care,
And kept them soft and sweet,
And fondly nursed and fed us there,
With pudding, milk and meat.

She sympathised with every one,
And made each case her own;
She had a heart for mirth and fun,
A tear for every groan.

Her smiles were sweet, her tears were warm,
Her bosom knew no guile;
She lived and moved to cheer and charm
The weak, the poor, the vile.

I never shall forget the day,
She ran and said "good-bye"
I shed some tears along the way,
Don't ask me where, nor why.

Bless me! How swift the years roll round!
She's twenty-one today!
As sweet as May, and I'll be bound
She's waiting for my lay.

Oh! May her future path be bright,
Undimmed by storm or shade,
And Angels guide to realms of light
The merry-orphan maid!

Wells Journal, July 1869

OUR CONVALESCENT COOK

Come all you skinny, pale-faced mortals come!
And fill your crops and feel yourselves at home,
Our bright eyed cook prepares five meals a day
And smiles to see us all stow them away.

Oh she can roast a joint and dress a steak,
And rhubarb pies and apple dumplings make,
She never lets the beef or bacon burn,
And does her chops and cutlets to a turn.

Upon the bread she lays butter thick
And always boils her eggs to please the sick,
The treacle on the cake she nicely spreads,
And sends us will full bellies to our beds.

Oh, she's a jolly, rosy, merry soul
As ever cracked a nut or fried a sole,
We love to hear her voice, so shrill and clear
And always feel at home when she is near.

Long may she live to boil and bake and roast,
To brew her tea and butter well her toast,
And comfort, feed and fatten those who come,
To rest and laugh and live in our sweet Home.

Wells Journal, July 1869

PRETTY POLLY

Dear Poll! though far from thee,
Thy form I seem to see,
Thy ringing laugh still charms my listening ear;
And oh, thy plumage bright,
I see by day and night,
And fondly fancy thou art ever near.

Oh! we were friends indeed!
No coaxing did'st thou need
To leave thy cage, and perch upon my hand,
Or stand upon my chair,
And talk and pull my hair,
While I was thinking on thy native land.

I fancied I could see,
Thee in thy island free,
With thousands more, where trees were ever green,
Where fruits and spices grew,
And skies were clear and blue,
And untrod forests grand, adorned the scene.

And oft at even-tide,
When sitting by thy side,
And listening to thy quiet, pensive lay,
Have I imagined thee,
Moaning to be set free,
And pining for they birth-land far away.

On bush, and brake, and tree,
I dearly love to see
The songsters wild, and hear their native songs;
But cages I detest
Mourn o'er the plundered nest,
And weep when musing on the warbler's wrongs.

I'd rather see them come
And take the offered crumb,
Dropped on the ground beside the bower or briar,
Than watch them tear and try
To gain their liberty,
Though kindly fed through bars of silver wire.

Let Polly walk the lawn,
And laugh and pick her bone
Among the flowers that gem her fair domain,
Or pace the green-house warm,
And every inmate charm
With native notes, and loving words again.

Farewell my pretty Poll!
Whene'er I take a stroll,
Sweet memories of thy fondness come to me,
Refreshing as the breeze
That comes from flowery leas,
And bind me closer to thy Home and thee.

Wells Journal, July 1869

THE PLOUGH

God speed the plough, and bless the hands
That till the fruitful earth,
There's not on this green land a gem
So bright as honest worth.
Let those who plough the emerald sod,
Or break the stubborn soil,
Look up with hope and Providence
Will bless their humble toil.

Nor let the sturdy ploughman shrink
From learning all he can;
For 'tis a truth endorsed by all,
"Tis mind that makes the man;"
And though the hands are hard with toil,
And flushed the manly brow,
It matters not, for God will bless
The labours of the plough.

Where'er the glittering ploughshare gleams
Beneath the sunny sky,
The tender blade and ripening ear
Are sure to greet the eye;
And waving fields, and golden sheaves,
The ploughman's hope and pride,
Crown the bright promise of the Spring
At coming Autumn-tide.

Though lowly be the ploughman's lot,
His honest heart is light,
Blest with the song of birds by day,
And sweet repose by night.
The dewdrops sparkle at his feet,
The flowers before him bow,
And every zephyr bears its prayer
For blessings on the plough.

The ploughman is a merry wight,
He turns the soil and sings,
And, while he earns his crust, he feels
The joy contentment brings;
He knows the precious seed he sows
Will rear the golden mow,
And rich and poor unite to bless
The labours of the plough.

Wells Journal, August 1869

POOR OLD PRIMROSE

Oh! Primrose, dost thou feel at home,
Among the lame and sick,
And do they ever jerk thy rein,
And thump thee with a stick?
Or shake thy poor old weary legs
Upon the fresh stoned road,
And make thy shoulders stiff and sore,
When tugging at thy load?

Oh! canst thou mind that sultry say
When Fred, and Frank rode out,
And one-legged Bill got up to drive
And strewed them all about,
Bruised and discoloured Fred's lame foot,
And gave Bill's knee a slap,
While noisy Frank, with his stiff knee,
Escaped without a rap?

And canst thou mind the narrow ditch
Along the Uphill road,
Where thou wast pitched upon thy back
Beside thy scattered load?
Ah! no, thou never canst forget
Thy tumble 'mongst the stumps,
When they upset the ambulance,
And got such stunning thumps.

And didst thou feel the nettles sting,
And are thy sides got well,
And do they feed thee well with corn,
And call thee with the bell?
And hast thou cropped the herbage bare,
Out in thy feeding ground,
And art thou shaded from the sun
Scorching the flowers around?

And do they give thee water pure,
When thou art parched with thirst,
And canst thou blow thy pipes as loud
As when I heard thee first?
And does the cook prepare thy meals
And pat thy head and sides,
And does the gardener keep the time,
When females take their rides?

Four hours a day, the Doctor said,
Were quite enough for thee
To wear the harness on thy back,
And so it seems to me:
Yet some would ride from morn to night,
And drive thee blind and lame,
Till thy friend Charles rose up and said
It was a burning shame.

Oh! do they keep thy feet well shod,
And brush thy old grey coat,
And give thee, now and then, a bean,
And treat thee as they ought?
Poor Prim! thou hast been knocked about,
As every body knows;
But He who note's the sparrow's fall,
Has numbered all thy blows.

And grasping, vice-stained, cruel-men,
Who swear, and smite, and kick,
And over-load the patient brute,
And make it faint and sick,
May one day knock at Heaven's gate
Ans wish the bolts withdrawn,
And then find out that mercy ne'er
Was meant for hearts of stone.

Shepton Mallet Journal, August 1869

TO A DEAR FRIEND'S FIRSTBORN SON

Hail smiling stranger, born,
Upon an April morn!
I'll greet thee with a song
The primrose banks among,
And wish thee every good
Beside the greening wood.

For thee the warblers sing
Blest babe of budding spring!
For thee the fragrant flowers
Perfume the boughs, the bowers,
And every bush and tree
Is dressing babe for thee!

And every bird and beast
In robes of beauty dressed,
That flutter o'er thy way
Or flock the meadows gay,
Before thee smiling rise
To charm thy opening eyes.

May thy enclosed brow,
Be ever bright as now,
Thy life be pure as fair,
Sweet child of hope and prayer,
And all thy coming days,
Be spent in wisdoms ways!

And may the God of love,
From His high throne above,
Smile on thee, Firstborn Boy,
Fill thy warm heart with joy,
And guide thee with his light,
To realms that know no sight.

Wells Journal, September 1869

154

CHRISTIAN CHARITY

How often do our preachers say,
"The path to heaven is steep,"
While bigots strew the way with thorns,
And make the Pilgrims weep!
And heaven-born souls are doomed to groan
Beneath the creed-worn rod,
Of those who intercept the way,
That leads to heaven and God.

No matter what the sect, 'tis creed,
Alone, that rules the roost,
And those who mangle hearts the best,
Are oft esteemed the most.
A man my wear an angel's form,
And all his deeds be pure;
This only makes the matter worse,
The poisoned shaft more sure.

'Tis "No Methodist need apply"
"No Churchmen wanted here"
Though not expressed in written words,
We meet with everywhere,
"We're going to heaven, you're going to hell,
You must adopt our rules;
The only passage to the skies,
Is through our training schools."

Of odds and ends of Bible-lore,
They have indeed their share;
But not a spark of Bible-love
Have their cold hearts to spare.
The golden rule they never learn,
But sneer and growl with all their might,
And fain would compass heaven and earth,
To make on Proselyte.

I knew a pious tradesman once,
An honour to the town,
Whose deeds of mercy and of love
Deserved the patriot's crown,
Far from his happy nest,
He left the town a ruined man
A wanderer after rest.

I knew a pure-souled maiden too,
Whose virtues brightly shone,
Sent weeping from a rich man's gate,
Because she dared to own,
A soul that soared towards the skies,
And nobly claimed the right,
To worship at a different shrine,
The Lord of life and light.

We know "the path to heaven is steep,"
Then why not join your hands,
And smoothen o'er the rugged way,
Ye fierce discordant bands?
There is a home among the stars,
From meddling mortals free,
There is a God that ever smiles
On love and unity.

Wells Journal, September 1869

POOR JACK

I saw in durance vile one day,
An Ass unfed with grass or hay,
And wondering what transgression black,
Had brought this evil on poor Jack,
I thus addressed the quiet brute,
Who listened with attention mute:

"Whose field hast thou been rambling o'er,
And from its banks the violets tore?
Whose hedges green hast thou despoiled,
Bedecked with honeysuckles wild?
Whose Close hast thou been cropping bare,
Destroying all the daisies there?
Oh, say what hast thou done, poor beast!
To be thus by misfortune chased?
Thou'rt dumb, but yet thou seemest to say,"

"Though in the pound I'm forced to stay
Till my hard master ope's the door,
I've done no harm at all, I'm sure;
I've never known one happy day,
Since with my Dam I used to stray,
I then could gambol, prance, and kick,
Oft feasting on the new-made rick,
And caper o'er the breezy down,
Nor care for pound nor mortal's frown.

In fertile fields below I fed,
With fragrant clover for my bed,
And there I watched the orchards bloom,
And breathed the cowslip's sweet perfume.
But all those rosy hours are flown,
And now ill-used, I'm doomed to groan.

To coal-pit yesterday I went,
And with the load my back was bent,
Galled o'er with burdens borne before,
Came home sick, weary, lame and sore;
These gory marks along my back
Made deeper by the hard coal-sack,
Proclaim the treatment I have borne
Since I've the yoke of bondage worn;
And ne'er, it seems, has Pity's face
Beamed on me, or my tortured race,
Save when in honoured days of yore,
The Saviour of mankind I bore,
The lightest, yet a weight divine,
E'er borne by beast of Palestine!

157

When faint and tired, at evening's close,
I need refreshment and repose,
My master then no kindness shows,
Nor gives me clover, oats, or tares,
Nor any kind of food prepares,
But drives me out in thoughtless haste,
To forage on the thorny waste,
And should I e'er the boundary scale,
Which bars me from the grassy vale,
And enter some warm sheltered close,
Where fresh, luxuriant herbage grows,
The wrathful owner comes with speed,
Before I've scarce enjoyed the feed,
Armed with a stout, uplifted stick,
And drives me through the fences thick.

Last evening late, with toil o'er wrought,
A supper in the lane I sought,
And breathing free the balmy air,
Thought no-one would molest me there.
Vain thought! a wretch who seemed insane,
Came striding down the quiet lane,
Called me "vile brute" and stamped and swore,
And kicked my sides till they were sore,
Then round my neck a briar placed,
And roared, "come on you ugly beast."
I followed; to the pound he led me,
And then forgot to feed or bed me.
Since then neglected here I've been,
Endured the pangs of hunger keen,
Wishing the weary day would close,
And night bring with it sweet repose."

Moved by the starving brute's appeal,
I threw it o'er an ample meal,
Relieved my bosom with a sigh,
And felt a tear bedim my eye.

Go, then! Ye sons of wisdom go!
Awhile your selfish schemes forego,
Go! ponder on the lesson taught,
And treat God's creatures as ye ought;
Remembering, He who made you knows
Their pangs, and numbers all your blows.

Shepton Mallet Journal, October 1869

TO A VIOLET

Emblem fair of modest worth
Peeping from the chilly earth
While the wintry blast is biting
And the sky is frowning o'er thee,
I hail thy advent early
Begemmed with dewdrops pearly
I loved thee when a boy
And now greet thee with a poet's joy!

Dearer to me thou art
Than the polished gems of art
So often dangled in my sight
For thou appearest with a smile
That yields the musing hearts delight
Charming the soul devoid of guile
Bringing back scenes of life gone by
When life was new, long, long ago
Without a care, without a foe.

Oh! thou precious little gem
I'll touch not thy slender stem
Nor tear away a single leaf
Beneath the sheltering holly tree,
Bloom sweetly through thy season brief,
And shed thy rich perfume for me
While the Robin woos his mate
From yonder orchard gate
Or tells his tender tales of love
Upon the naked boughs above.

Wells Journal, February 1870

WINTER

Old Winter, with his frosty face,
Now hovers o'er the land and main,
And chilling upland breezes sweep
The brave old forest oaks again;
And while the blast howls wild
Against the humble cottage door,
Oh! may the generous and the kind
Relieve the brave, but suffering poor.

The favoured sons of wealth, we know,
Have blazing hearths and beds of down,
And they can gaily pass the hours,
And smile serene at Winter's frown;
But while the drifting snow descends,
And covers o'er the level moor,
Oh! may the feeling and the kind,
Have pity on the suffering poor.

Ye little know the trails of those,
Who toil beneath the open sky,
Exposed to every icy blast
That bends the back, or blinds the eye;
Yet, these we know, have hearts as pure
And warm, as England's high-born dons,
Make both ends meet, and pay their way
As well as Fashion's favoured sons.

The vices of the "Upper Ten"
We see recorded very day,
Ne'er crimsoned o'er their honest brows,
Nor stamped with shame their coarser clay,
All honour to our toilers then,
On lake and land or factory floor!
May the Great Giver bless them all,
And shower his blessings on the poor!

And may the glorious task be sweet
To those whose coffers overflow,
To cheer the hamlet and the town,
And soothe the sons of want and woe;
And, oh! ye happy heaven-born souls,
Besiege the gates of Heaven once more,
And let your warmest prayers ascend,
For blessings on the suffering poor.

Wells Journal, February 1870

EARLY IMPRESSIONS

How charmingly the past comes back
Again before the joy-lit eye,
When fancy runs in childhood's track
Along beneath a summer sky!
The mossy bank and rippling stream
Have faces quite as bright to-day
As when, beneath the noon-tide beam,
I rolled upon the meadow hay.

I seem to see the flowers again,
The buttercup and the primrose pale,
That blossomed in the shady lane,
That led me to the open dale;
And I can see the daisies now,
That fringed my lonely path to school,
Where Polly sang and milked her cow,
And capered round the milking stool.

I see the beech trees, where the flock
Sought shelter form the scorching beam,
Above the rain-washed, breeze-swept rock
Beside the pathway to the stream;
Where I have seen the maidens run,
Adown the hill towards the well;
And watched at eve the setting sun,
Declining o'er the lovely dell.

The skylark's song trilled in the morn,
The cuckoo's note in early Spring,
The blackbird's anthem on the thorn,
The hum of insects on the wing,
Ah, all are sweet and fresh to me,
As when, with smooth and sunny brow,
I whistled o'er the furrowed lea,
And drove the team before the plough.

The monarch oak beside the wood,
The shady walk along the grove,
The ivy, where the old mill stood,
The silent rhine beside the drove,
Appear, by turns, before my eye,
All-glorious as in days of yore;
The hours of childhood never die,
Though future ones return no more.

The stream that sweetly murmurs by,
The corn that waves upon the down,
The hum of toil in village nigh,
The tear and turmoil of the town,
Are just the same they ever were;
The steam will flow, the corn field wave,
And hamlets hum and cities wear,
When I am silent in the grave.

Wells Journal, March 1870

LILLIE GREEN

When I go musing round the town,
What merry maidens do I see,
Fair as the daisies on the down,
Or violets on the verdant lea!
Some dressed in black and some in white,
And some in different shades between,
Yet, none gives me so much delight,
As smiling Lillie Green.

Her face is round and rather pale,
Her loving eyes are soft and clear,
Her rose-bud lips can tell a tale,
That oft has charmed my listening ear;
In the full glory of her youth,
Her sunny number just sixteen,
And full of life, and love, and truth,
Is charming Lillie Green.

Oh! She's a gem beside the hearth,
As sweet and sunny as the day,
And you may estimate her worth,
When you can count the buds of May;
I've seen her at the close of day,
As merry as a May-day Queen,
And often thought when far away,
On cheerful Lillie Green.

I often sigh to think that I
Was born so many years ago;
But what's the use to fret and sigh,
Or rack my brain about her so?
Yet I must own, and frankly, too,
'Mongst all the maidens I have seen,
There's none, I think, would love so true,
As loving Lillie Green.

And blest indeed will be the swain,
Who wins her priceless heart and hand;
I'll greet him with a merry strain,
And may it echo through the land!
The bloom of youth may disappear,
And time's footprints be dimly seen,
But life can ne'er be dull or drear,
With happy Lillie Green.

Cornubian and Redruth Times, September 1870

163

THE SOLDIER'S BETROTHED

'Neath India's burning sky
The warrior heaves a sigh
To tread his far-off fatherland again
That fair old Isle of Isles
Where freedom ever smiles,
And waves her banner o'er the land and main.

His birth land far away
He views by night and day
With all its sunny spots, its downs and dells
Its ancient temple towers
Its ivy mantled bowers
Its singing stream and moss clad crystal walls.

And in a lowly cot
That ne'er will be forgot
He sees the lass he loved long years ago,
Fond playmates then they were
They breathed their vows sincere
And felt more blessed than larger lovers know.

Then Carrie's parents died
Her friendship scattered wide
Her lover sailed for India's Coral Strand
Yet scarce a tear she shed
While toiling for her bread
But seemed the happiest mortal in the land.

And still she toils and sings
And to the wind she flings
The thoughts that oft would shade her sunny brow,
As the days roll on
She counts the number gone
And lives by faith upon her lover's vow.

Sing on fair maid! Each day
That slowly rolls away
Leaving faint traces on thy smiling face
Will surely bring at last
The hour to heal the past
And from thy breast each anxious feeling chase.

Safe o'er the storm tossed main
May he return again
To be her loving playmate as of yore,
When in the flush of youth
Each uttered word was truth
And very vow the stamp of nature bore!

Ye hours speed fast away
And bring their meeting day
And let me greet them with a loving lay
And then the birds will sing
And angels sweetly smile
On Carrie's wedding day.

Wells Journal, October 1870

RAIN

The rain, rain, rain,
How it beats against the window pane,
Now it glideth, now it gushes,
Or it ripples, or it rushes,
'Twixt the fitful breaks and brushes
Of the wind's refrain.

Oh! rain, rain, rain
Art thou weeping for the slain?
For the sunny summer hours
We shall never see again;
There's a warning in thy moan
A mystery in thy tone,
And more than all, a sadness
Of a kind akin to pain.

Oh! rain, rain, rain
Thou hast reason to complain,
But not to sob despairingly,
Or cry, that hope is vain,
Then, brief outcast from the skies,
Soon again to them shall rise;
Would so might all thou art falling on
Tonight, oh! rain, rain, rain.

Wells Journal, October 1870

THE WATER QUESTION[21]

The "Water Question" what a tempting theme
For City Scribes without a home or name;
"The water's pure" and "we've got a good supply"
Our scientific men in New Street cry:
While others meet them with a stern retort,
"The water's always bad and sometimes short.
We know the water's bad we've tried it years enough."
And yet we daily have to use the wretched stuff.
Whence comes the water that supplies our wells,
Not from the Mendips or the neighbouring dells,
Dig in the gravelly soil where'er you like
The water flows, a spring you're sure to strike:
But you may search and dig until you're blind,
No genuine springs in Wells you'll ever find.
The soil receives the rain and the clouds pour down,
This makes the cistern which supplies the town:
But what becomes of all the filth that lies
In nooks and corners hidden from our eyes,
The oozings from the dungheap and the styes,
From cess pools reeking 'neath the open skies
From slaughter houses stained with stinking blood,
And all the gas the churchyard has to spare,
From countless corpses rotting there?
Why it goes down to keep the cistern full
To make it pure and bright and beautiful!
And every little dog that lifts its leg,
And swills the grocer's chest or brewer's keg
And every cat that hurries to the wall,
Obedient to Dame Nature's constant call,
Helps to fill up the reservoir below,
It matters little whether swift or slow,
Along with every other stinking thing,
To feed with filth our far-famed City Spring!
And then we pump the precious mixture up,

---

[21] Bishop Bekynton granted the use of the water of Wells to the people in 1451; they drew water from the conduit in the Market Place and gulleys either side the city's main street. However, as the town and its population grew during the Victorian age the quality of the water deteriorated and was a cause of distress to the working population, who demanded cleaner water and access throughout the city.

To fill the kettle, the breakfast cup:
Into the dinner pot it likewise goes,
And who can estimate the harm it does?
And yet we hear our native wise ones cry
"Our shallow gravel pits are never dry,
And what's the use of making such a fuss
Our own well-water's good enough for us."
While close at hand the sparkling crystal rills,
Are ever gushing from the Mendip Hills,
Our busy local board blocks up the way,
By telling us things will never pay,
And let the precious streamlet run to waste,
So clear, so pure and pleasant to the taste
But yet, in spite of all that learned men
May say, or scheme, or plan with lip and pen
In spite of all their obstructive band can do
Backed by their Champion's clever Chaplain too,
We soon shall see the metal pipes laid down,
And pure spring water flowing through the town;
Then will our City brewers make good beer
A thing that was never manufactured here,
The water butt will then be thrown aside,
For softer water running by its side,
And every baker work with sweeter yeast
And every quartern have a better taste.
No factories then will luminate the skies,
Out goes the plugs, up the water flies
No pumps be wanted, and no soles worn out,
By maidens running to the conduit spout;
No begging water then when wells are dry,
No locking pumps from thirsty neighbours nigh,
And every family man will bless the day
The deep, pure springs of Mendip flowed this way.

Wells Journal, November 1870

THE ARTFUL RUSTIC

One sunny morn a Parson shorn,
And trimmed from top to toe completely,
Walked forth at ease 'neath shady trees,
Absorbed in thought, and wondering greatly.

How 'twas that men should now and then,
Forget to recompense him duly,
Since he had taught them as he ought,
And told them all their errors truly.

'Twas hard he felt that so much thought,
And constant labour should be wasted;
For in the shade he'd Sermon's made,
And for their sakes had prayed and fasted.

At length, he saw a cottage low,
Marked well its little garden blooming,
And witnessed there the rustic's care,
And saw his bees their toil resuming.

He gazed, and lo! in one long row,
Ten hives of bees he reckoned;
Yes, they were there, he saw them clear,
And to the owner straightway beckoned.

John doffed his tile, and with a smile
The rosy Rector kindly greeted;
"Why, bless me, John, how you get on,
While I am daily wronged and cheated!

I've come to ease you of some bees,
For surely you've a hive too many;
You've ten, I see, and one to me
Belongs, for I have scarcely any."

The Rector ceased, his mind he'd eased;
But John looked gloomy on the Pastor;
He wished him dead, but calmly said,
"I'll bring them to you in the evening Master."

A lucky thought on John wrought,
It made him smile, it was so funny;
The scheme was deep, the hive he'd keep,
And give the bees without the honey.

When evening came, John played his game,
And managed well his bit of scheming,
Took o'er the bees with perfect ease,
With pleasure on his features beaming.

The Rector's door he reached secure,
And quite elated with his notion,
Into the hall with bees and all,
He rushed, and set the swarm in motion.

The hive is mine, the bees are thine,
He cried, and quickly retreated;
While the whole swarm in dire alarm,
Were quickly on the Parson seated.

The Servants squalled, the Rector bawled,
And all appeared like persons crazy;
John closed the door, and said, I'm sure
You've got my bees, I hope they'll please ye.

Worcestershire Chronicle, September 1871

THE POET'S WALK[22]

North from the spirit-fretting town,
In rosy Spring's fresh morning hour,
O'er glittering glade and golden down,
Towards his dear old native bower,
The musing poet tripped along,
The dewdrops glistened on the flowers,
The merry birds were full of song;
How lovely seemed this earth of ours.

Toward that home of homes he sped,
Where light first danced upon his brow,
Where first he pressed the downy bed,
And watched the robin on the mow;
Where he first tumbled on the sod,
And gambolled 'midst the heath and thyme,
Knelt down before his father's God,
And breathed in orisons his rhyme.

Loved pictures of life's early days
In fancy's mirror brightly shone;
'Twas there he trilled his happiest lays,
And carolled when his toil was done;
And there his parents' virtues bloomed,
Like flowers where sheltering hedges rise,
And all their daily deeds perfumed
With fragrance borrowed from the skies.

There concord reigned the live-long day,
No cares disturbed their sweet repose;
And life seemed like the sunset ray
That gilds a summer evening's close;
The Holy Book, the pilgrim's guide
To mansions in the realms of light
They conned at morn and eventide,
And lingered o'er its precepts bright.

---

[22] Catcott suggested that John Harris enter one of his poems in the national Shakespeare Tercentenary Poetry Competition in April 1864, which he won and was awarded a gold watch. Later that year, Catcott received and the *Wells Journal* printed the following letter from Harris: "A few weeks ago I visited my birthplace. The dear old croft I have written so much about and love so well is now ploughed up and converted into a field of corn. When I saw the green oats waving in the breeze and mused on happy hours of rhyming passed in my mossy bower, now mine no longer and stripped to me of all its inspiration, the heath and thyme all rooted up and burnt in the fire, I sat down and shed many tears. …Change comes to all sublunary things and the poet as well as the politician is forgotten in the rush of the world after gain. I write this letter to you thinking my desolate bower would be a nice subject for your pen".

And there Dame Nature piled her rocks
And crags in grandeur wild around,
Washed with the sea her granite blocks,
And hid her wealth beneath the ground;
And beautified with primrose dells,
And sunny slopes, and hills gold-crowned,
And mosses bright, and heather-bells,
His birth-land, and his training-ground.

Such was the home, and such the scenes
That cheered and charmed his early hours;
And years before he passed his teens
He wooed the Muse in Nature's bowers:
Portrayed, with wondrous grace and skill,
The depths and dangers of the mine,
That tuned his lyre, beside the rill,
And sweetly trilled his songs divine.

And now he stands upon the spot,
Gemmed with the primrose and the thorn,
The daisy and forget-me-not,
Where he, the best of bards, was born;
But Mammon's hand had changed the scene,
The restless plough the croft had torn,
And where he sought the mosses green,
His eyes beheld the waving corn.

The footprints of Time's march he saw
Impressed upon his old domain,
And hill and heath and valley low,
Bore traces of the thirst for gain;
And, musing there on days gone by,
He watered with his tears the sod,
Relived his bosom with a sigh,
And bowed before a changeless God.

Morning Musings (1870)

THE EARLY PRIMROSE

Beneath the frowning yew
A lovely primrose grew;
And sweetly blossomed there,
'Midst winter's frosts severe.
In cold December's gloom
It opened like a bloom,
And like a star it shone,
In beauty, all alone.

I watched the precious gem
Upon its tiny stem,
Within its leafy nest,
And hailed the welcome guest;
And every time I passed,
It smiled upon the waste,
And beautified the spot
Beside my humble cot.

So genius shed its rays,
In trial's bitterest days,
And gems of brilliant thought,
Are to perfection brought.
Though thorns may choke the way,
And storm clouds shade the day,
The mind displays its might,
And bears its blossoms bright.

So Virtue, like the flower,
In Life's tempestuous hour,
Uprears her Angel-form,
And braves the raging storm
Watched by a loving eye
Above the starry sky,
And screened from every harm
By an Almighty arm.

Morning Musings (1870)

APRIL

Welcome green April, fresh and fair,
With floral wreaths upon thy brow,
Diffusing fragrance through the air,
And life into each bud and bough!

Thy mornings fresh, thy evenings clear,
With now and then a genial shower
From clouds with silver-edges near,
Tinting with green each bush and bower.

How sweet the opening violets smell
Along the bank beside the copse,
While buttercups, like golden bells,
Allure us to the sunny slopes.

And primroses sweet memories bring,
Shedding, it seems a hallowed light
On bank and bush and everything,
When day is gliding into night.

And dotting dingle, down and dell,
The daisy shines through sun-warmed tears,
And on the paths, though trodden well,
An ever-smiling aspect wears.

Each day the landscape greener grows,
The hedges don their spring-tide vest,
And every hour fresh beauty shows,
And brighter sunsets gem the west.

Between the clouds, how blue the sky,
Now heaven's bright bow had passed away;
And while the zephyr's softly sigh,
The blackbird trills his evening lay.

And soon, among the elms below,
The apple trees with blossoms crowned,
With all their wealth of beauty show,
And make the heart with gladness bound.

Oh! April, smiling through thy tears,
We love thy changing, charming face;
In everything thy hand uprears,
Our Father's skill and care we trace.

Morning Musings (1870)

CORNISH VIOLETS

From some warm Western dell,
These violets come to tell
Again, their cheering tale that spring is near,
Whispering of meadows green,
Where bursting buds are seen,
And milkmaids' notes are ringing strong and clear.

And oh! before my mind
They bring a maiden kind,
Sweeter and fairer than the summer rose;
I've gazed upon her face,
Down in her native place,
And met her where the purple heather grows.

Beside her in the train,
I've rattled o'er the plain,
And watched the trees and hedges dance along,
And once 'twas our sweet lot
To find a poet's cot,
Beside the sea, and listen to his song.

Swift flew the summer hours,
We spent among the flowers,
That gemmed the loving poet's fair domain,
And so much kindness rare
Was lavished on us there,
I fear we ne'er shall share the like again.

Dark clouds are shading now
My weary aching brow,
And wasting sickness, with her humbling hand,
Has swept away the flowers
That decked life's earlier hours,
And left me hoping for a better land.

Yet still down in the West
My spirit yearns to rest,
Where loving hearts and kindred spirits dwell;
And by some rippling rill,
Near Ellen's dear old hill,
My aching heart would sigh its last farewell.

Morning Musings (1870)

STANZAS TO A FRIEND
ON RECEIVING SOME PRIMROSES IN A LETTER

Precious token of goodwill,
Gathered near some rippling rill,
Offerings pure from Friendship's hand,
From the far-off Western land;
Welcome to my humble bower,
Every crushed and crumbled flower.

Bright the memories ye bring,
Sweet the fragrances that he fling,
Chasing with your presence gay,
Harping business cares away;
Welcome then, ye spring-tide gems,
With your bruised and battered stems.

Heart's thanks from a heart brim-full,
For earth's stars are so beautiful,
Coming up fresh with the dew,
From the meadow where ye grew,
Near the sunny sea-washed hill,
Where the waves are never still.

Dear to me your yellow eyes,
Opened 'neath the Cornish skies,
Where my loving friends reside,
Where the poet and his bride,
And your giver, young and fair,
Cheer me with their kindness rare.

Shall I ever see again
The gold-crowned knoll above the plain,
Daisy-dotted, where ye bloom,
Near the heather and the broom,
Where your donor's cottage stand,
And the tide o'erflows the strand?

When the bee begins to hum,
When the days of Summer come,
Oh! I then may run away,
And spend one happy day,
With a fair and faithful friend,
Smiling near the famed Land's End.

Morning Musings (1870)

TO MARY

When shall I climb the hills, or tread
The flowery fields with thee again,
Together on the mountain's head,
Admire the beauties of the plain,
Or stand upon the sunny strand,
And breathe the breeze that fans the land?

In concord sweet, our souls breathed forth
Their deep emotions as they rose;
We talked of authors and their worth,
Commended friends and pitied foes,
And gaily spent the evenings fair,
Unclouded by a thought or care.

And when the moon in beauty rose,
Illuming with her mellow ray,
The dying evening's soft repose,
We calmly mused the hours away,
Disclosing all we felt, and thought
That friendship's ties were firmly wrought.

Adown the lane, or by the stream,
Across the vale, or o'er the heath,
Where're we walked, a holy gleam
From heaven seemed gilding all beneath,
Chastening each feeling of the breast,
And soothing every thought to rest.

The memory of those rambles dear,
Lies buried deep within my breast,
And while I sigh, oppressed with care,
My lonely spirit feels no rest;
How sweetly flew those golden hours,
With thee among the summer flowers.

Farewell, ye sunny moments dear!
I cannot hope for your return;
Farewell, bright spot in life's career!
To the dark future now I turn,
But scarce a gleam of Hope's bright ray,
Breaks forth to cheer the coming day.

Morning Musings (1870)

177

AN ODE TO JOHN HARRIS,
THE CORNISH POET

All hail! sweet minstrel of the west!
Thou Prince of Bards, of men the best!
I'll greet thee with a homely lay,
And trill a grateful song today.
Methinks thy native hills and dells,
Which oft have thrown their magic spells
Around thy poet-soul, will ring
A sweeter strain than I can sing;
And streams will ripple out a line,
And with the voiceful glens combine,
To chaunt their most delightful lays,
And sing aloud their votary's praise.
Nor will the woodland silent be,
For every leaf on every tree
Will lisp in they enraptured ear,
A lyric such as poets hear;
And every pasture, path and plain,
And sunny nook and shaded lane,
And breezy down and bushy brake,
And mossy bank and mist-crowned lake,
Shall music to thy spirit breathe,
And true poetic chaplets wreathe,
For thee, thou taught in Nature's school
Thou lover of the beautiful!

Sweet poet of the dewy dells!
I hail thee 'mongst the heather-bells,
And in the cells where misery dwells,
Where pinching want its history tells,
And vice, in all its hideous hues,
Its headstrong downward course pursues.
With thee I penetrate the gloom
That settles round the outcast's room,
And see thee like a prophet stand,
And point towards the better land;
I see thee, O, thou poet-priest!
Dispelling with thy light the mist
That shrouds the slumbering sinner's eye
I see the tear and mark the sigh,
And greet thee as the poet-guide
Of wanderers to the crucified;
And hail thee as a genius bright,
Reposing on fame's laureled height.

Sweet poet of the mount and mine!
I hail thee as a bard divine,
And con they lyrics with delight,
Feasting upon thy fancies bright,
And linger o'er the fancies bright,
And linger o'er each jewelled line
That gems thy melodies divine.
Rich with the wealth thy muse has culled,
From meadow, mountain, waste and wold;
They sparkle like the singing brook
When gushing from some fairy-nook
The sunbeam dances on its crest,
And showers its diamonds on its breast.

And when I listen to thy lyre
Beside the Sabbath evening fire,
The music of its love-toned notes
Then sweetly mingle with my thoughts,
And soothing as an angels hymn,
Its warblings to my spirit seem.
Fain would I to thy mantle cling,
And soar with thee on Fancy's wing,
Until my soul, like thine, was full
Of fancies pure and beautiful,
Till every wayward thought of mine
Became as bright and pure as thine.

Morning Musings (1870)

179

THE NEW YEAR

The midnight bells are ringing
Out the old decaying year,
And to the memory bringing
Thoughts of gladness and care;
Whilst solemn truths are sinking
Deep into the heart anew;
The past and present linking
In the lonely spirit's view.

The scenes are daily shifting,
As we trip along life's road,
As onward we are drifting
To the spirit-land of God,
And may our cares be lighter,
As the new year rolls along,
And all our prospects brighter,
Till we end it with a song!

In heaven's goodness trusting,
Let us use the hand and pen,
And keep our powers from rusting
By an effort now and then,
To make our light more shining,
And our morals brighter too,
The inner man refining
With the beautiful and true.

Bright spirits watching o'er us,
Jotting down each glorious thought,
Soar to the skies before us,
And record the good we've wrought.
Our errors, too, are noted,
Every sin and moral stain,
And every whim that floated
Through the region of the brain.

Our lives are ever preaching
To the old and to the young,
And good or evil teaching,
By the conduct on the tongue.
Oh! let us then be stirring
In this world of war and strife;
We may reclaim the erring,
And enhance the joys of life.

So onward moving ever
Let us adorn life's pages,
And hopefully endeavour
To shine in future ages.
Aye, walk the earth, and startle
Every slumbering soul we find,
Till we become immortal
In the glorious realm of mind.

Morning Musings (1870)

OBITUARY

Mr. William Catcott, affectionately known in this city as The Baker Bard of Wells, and author of numerous poems died at his residence in Tor Street last Sunday.

The Baker Bard was well-known and had been a contributor to this Journal from the commencement of his career and many have been the laughs and jokes that followed the effusions from his pen.

Many of his poems were often upon subjects of a local theme but his admiration of nature's floral gems and everything else unassuming which reflected upon his life and character to the highest degree featured in his verse.

That he was kindly disposed towards all his fellow creatures and ever ready to lend a helping hand to the sons and daughters of distress is fully testified by all those with whom he came in contact. His nature was altogether unselfish. He strove, as far as in him lay, to do unto others as he would be done by and we admire him as much as a man as a poet.

All things pure and good and beautiful in the moral and physical universe were appreciated by the self-taught Baker Bard who strove to elevate his countrymen by his life and song. Let it be remembered that William Catcott was a worker from his childhood to the time of his death.

If it had not been for his bodily strength giving way he might have continued for a long time to be a bright ornament amongst his literary friends and he was a highly respected neighbour amongst all who knew him.

Wells Journal, November 1870

INDEX OF FIRST LINES

A charming nurse indeed is Emily..143
A glorious picnic party? Bless my heart...73
A hearty cheer for those who find...82
All hail! sweet minstrel of the west...178
Among the apple trees..119
Another glorious gala day...76
Away! away! with speed away! 91
Away down in the sunny west...128
Away from Dorsetshire..86
Away ye sentimental bores...92
Behold! The grand procession's formed...115
Beneath the frowning yew..173
Beneath the verdant sod...37
Beside an honour'd parent's bier..16
Beside the Ocean's Foam..145
Bless me, you're going to London, eh?..88
Borne on the evening breeze the deep tonn'd knell..13
But yesterday he faced the oven's mouth..135
Can you pass the village church..64
Close beside the old wood pile...78
Come all you skinny, pale-faced mortals come!...148
Come, Christians, clear the crowded brow..63
Come praise the Lord for sun and shade..79
Dear Poll! Though far from thee...149
Did you ever think how noble...4
Down from the North the missive came...12
Emblem fair of modest worth..159
Enlightened herald of a glorious day...62
E're scarce the lingering light of day...19
Fair ever-welcome thing...124
For the warriors I plead, and hope not in vain..15
From dell and down, now haste away..75
From some warm Western dell..175
Go forth thou herald of a brighter day..3
God speed the plough..151
Hail smiling stranger, born...154
Hail thou glory of the spring! 60
Half the night, beside the day...108
Have mercy on the calves...141
Here comes young blustering March...139
How charmingly the past comes back..161
How fresh and gay comes charming May..113
How oft will gossips meet and prate..126
How often do our preachers say...155
How glorious is the summer time...27
How sweet the cowslips smell..129
I can't forget thee Kit!..48
I hope the baker's scribbling foes...107

I knew a jolly fellow, young and strong...53
I love the flowers, the marigolds..96
I love the quiet evening hour...113
I love to sing a maiden's birthday lay...67
I'll tune my lyre among the sheaves today..20
I'm sometimes sad, and yet I am calm..136
I met her at the water-side..146
I saw in durance vile one day..157
I see before my mind's eye, bright and clear...117
I see the empty chair..6
I thought I had a noble friend..45
It seems, sometimes, a blessing to be ill..134
I walked on eve beside the Palace Moat..90
Just twenty minutes driving down..84
Long have I gazed upon her charms..138
Long years of toil have rolled away...69
Lovely violets now are blooming...10
Mary! Thou precious gift today! 93
Merry maids in days gone by...30
Neath poplars high, beside a stream...32
Neath India's burning sky..164
"No Methodist need apply!"..58
No more upon the water clear..18
North from the spirit-fretting town...171
Now soothing is the welcome calm...106
Oh! a daisy blossom sweet..114
Oh! Bessy, let me sing a song..144
Oh! lay her gently, gently down..102
Oh! Primrose, dost that feel at home...152
Oh tell me not of dreary things..132
Oh! the light summer breeze..118
Oh, well! her happy spirit's fled..103
Oh! where are the fond ones I loved to have near me..125
Oh! where the stream flows o'er the pebbles clear..1
Old England! 'tis a glorious land...36
Old Winter, with his frosty face...160
One April morn I limped away..34
One sunny morn a parson shorn..169
On Sabbath evenings calm and lone...33
Our Floral Holiday!...71
Over the sunny southern hills..110
Precious token of goodwill...176
Seated chatting with a friend..112
Sing a song for sunny Sue...61
Stern duty calls, and I must leave..57
Sweetly birds are singing...68
Thanks, thanks for the flowers..65
The blessed morning light...54
The breeze blows fresh o'er Mendip's famous hills..120
The cold wind strips the yellow leaf..95

The day was cloudy, yet the breeze...25
The evening breeze is bringing...42
The last leaf quivers in the breeze..9
The midnight bells are ringing..180
The mist is hovering o'er the stream...94
The opening dawn the knell has rung..21
The rain beats hard against the window pane...81
The rain, the rain, the rain...166
The robin comes to pick the crumbs...99
The steam horse pants along the road...22
The "Water Question" what a tempting theme...167
There's lots of teasing men about..50
There is one spot to me more dear..7
There's something in a friendly tone...24
There's something in the twilight hour..8
They say that I'm a drunken beast...130
Thou'rt worn out now, old Barrow!...28
T'was after she became a bride...40
T'was when the nuts were getting brown..80
Two pilgrims on life's rugged road...47
Up in the light of sunny day...51
We buried her, t'was in the early spring..44
We love the plants that deck the lawns...56
We rise to guard our Fatherland..5
Welcome green April, fresh and fair...174
What means those bonfires bright...123
What memories the feelings greet...2
When clouds are low'ring o'er us...11
When I go musing round the town..163
When shall I climb the hills, or tread...177
Where noble elms their shadows throw..97
William! Wherever thou mayest be..43
Ye noble hearts with kindness swelling..121
Young John and Joan the papers say..100